CLASS ACT

HOW TO BEAT THE BRITISH CLASS SYSTEM

Lynda Lee-Potter

metro

First published in Great Britain in 2000
by Metro Books (an imprint of Metro Publishing Limited),
19 Gerrard Street, London W1V 7LA

The excerpts on pages 36 and 181 from 'How to Get On in Society'
by John Betjeman, from his Collected Poems, are reproduced by
kind permission of John Murray Publishers.

British Library Cataloguing in Publication Data.
A CIP record of this book is available on request from the British Library.

ISBN 1 900512 97 1

10 9 8 7 6 5 4 3 2 1

Typeset by MATS, Southend-on-Sea, Essex
Printed in Great Britain by CPD Group, Wales

CONTENTS

1
UPWARDLY MOBILE

People may sneer at me for writing a book about class. Some will insist class no longer exists and that it's an outmoded concept. Others will say that no one called Lynda from a working-class background has any right to pontificate on the subject. Actually, I can't think of anyone better equipped to do so, having trawled my way through more classes than most. I only discovered the true significance of class when I married into an upper-middle-class family but the subject has fascinated me ever since. I grew up in the small mining town of Leigh in Lancashire and almost everyone I knew in my childhood came from a similar background. I didn't even realize there was any other kind of cheese except white crumbly Lancashire.

Although I knew little about class differences when I was young, I always had ideas above my station. l yearned to be something I wasn't. I wanted to be one of those posh school-girls in Enid Blyton's 'Malory Towers' books. I wanted to live in a big detached house and I'd have sold my soul to play lacrosse and use words like 'spiffing' and 'super'. My mother longed for me to be pretty but I was fat and plain, with fine straight hair and thousands of freckles. All my childhood I remember people coming up to me and saying, 'You're Peggy Berry's girl aren't you? What a pity you're not pretty like your mother.' I always felt guilty, as though I'd let her down somehow, but she loved me totally and never stopped trying to combat nature. Money was tight, and at times she could barely afford the nine shillings and sixpence council rent, but she would have gone without food herself rather than be late with the payment. She was too proud to ever be in debt.

My parents met at a dance in Leigh parish church hall. They went to the Isle of Man for their honeymoon, which was considered incredibly smart in the days when most working-class couples from Lancashire went to Blackpool or Morecambe. My mother had film-star looks and was devastatingly pretty with stunning legs which she liked to show off in fiendishly high-heeled shoes. She worked in the Trueform shoe shop, and when my father first left school at fourteen, he began work as a coal miner in a Leigh colliery. He hated it so much he left after a few weeks and got a job as an apprentice to a painter and decorator. During my adolescence, my mother always said, 'Never tell anyone your daddy worked down the pit.'

When I became a journalist on the *Daily Mail*, I interviewed miners' leader Joe Gormley. He told me that people used to be ashamed of coming from a mining background. 'Now,' he said, 'it's something they're proud of.' In the end I was to feel the same way but it took me a shamingly long time to learn.

No one I knew in Leigh had a car except our GP Dr Harris who was a gentleman. He had much charm and always showed great courtesy to my family. The one quality possessed by those who have true class is that they treat all people with respect, be they employees, clients or patients. Dr Harris had two sons, Nicky and Colin, who, before they went away to boarding school, attended Leigh Parish Church Primary with me. Every morning he drove them to school and sometimes he'd see me walking along and stop and give me a lift. Our worlds were poles apart but I've never forgotten how he made me feel welcome and of value.

For the first year of my life we lived with my widowed grandfather. He was an ex-miner, a passionate socialist and his second home was Leigh Labour Club. The front door of his terraced house in Gordon Street opened onto the pavement, and the colliery where he worked all his life was a few minutes' walk away. There was a fish and chip shop on the corner and milk was delivered by horse and cart. Everyone went into the street with jugs to collect the milk which was poured from huge churns. Gambling was prohibited in those days but my granddad made a few shillings each week by betting on the dogs. An illegal runner called Benny came to the house for his money every Friday. Women wore aprons which were called pinnies and housework was hard and relentless. The front doorstep had to be scrubbed with pumice stone, the fire had to be made and the grate black-leaded. My granddad had no bathroom and only a cold-water tap in the kitchen. The washing was done in a huge boiler once a week and then hung over a clothes rack, which was suspended by pulleys from the front-room ceiling. I was deeply embarrassed by it, but when middle-class farmhouse kitchens were all the rage, clothes racks became fashionable. The house had no electricity, only fragile gas mantles which had to be lit with a match and which were forever breaking. The lavatory was at the bottom of the yard, and instead of lavatory paper, the *News Chronicle* was torn into neat squares and hung on a string.

When I was one year old, my mother heard that some new council houses were being built on the other side of Leigh and she went to the Town Hall to apply for one. She was a natural performer so she took with her the only book my granddad owned. It was the complete works of George Bernard Shaw and she thought it would demonstrate that she'd be a good tenant. I don't know if the book had any influence but she had overpowering sex appeal and could charm anyone – and she got the house. We moved in almost immediately and we stayed there until I was sixteen.

My mother was a born actress who undeniably had star quality and always liked to be the centre of attention. She'd had little formal education although, for some reason, she knew the entire speech from Shakespeare's *As You Like It*, beginning:

All the world's a stage,
And all the men and women merely players:
They have their exits and their entrances;
And one man in his time plays many parts . . .

It was particularly apt for her because she was a chameleon who truly did believe we all have to play different parts. 'People tell you to just be yourself,' she used to say, 'but I think it's better to be different depending who you're with.' My mother and I were never devotees of the philosophy that we should be natural. We were always trying to be better, playing out roles and trying to be what we thought was required.

She was a great party-giver who always made Christmas seem wondrous. My aunties and uncles would come round on Christmas Eve and we'd have a hotpot supper with slices of beetroot in vinegar. When I was first married and helping my mother-in-law Lady Lee Potter prepare salad for lunch, I said, 'Shall I slice the beetroot and put it in vinegar?' Giving a remarkable imitation of Lady Bracknell's handbag speech, she said in absolute horror, 'In *vinegar*?'

Every Christmas, my family played old-fashioned games

like Tippet and Who's There? and one game which involved sitting in a large group around a roaring fire and making up stories. Then my parents would do a soft-shoe shuffle and sing an emotional song called 'Another Year Has Passed Away'. Around midnight all the guests would leave and walk home through the silent, frosty streets linking arms and singing carols. My mother had a spartan upbringing but she always created warmth and luxury for me. She was only three years old when her mother died in childbirth. She and her sisters and brother were looked after by their eldest sister who, at eleven, virtually became mother and housekeeper. 'We weren't brought up,' my mother used to say, 'we just grew up.'

When I was eight years old, my mother opened a small wallpaper and paint shop in Leigh and, as she was an astute businesswoman, she turned it into a goldmine. She worked all hours, but Wednesday was half-day closing and it was the one day in the week she was at home when I got back from school. Every Wednesday she'd be standing at the open front door waiting for me as I walked down the street. In winter she'd have a huge fire burning, all the lamps in the sitting room switched on and warm homemade scones on the table.

I was probably the first child in Lancashire to have what was known as a 'permanent wave'. I went to the local hairdresser and was wired up to a six-foot perming machine for hours. Then, every night, my mother rolled up the resultant frizz in rags and put lemon juice on my freckles but my round, truculent face still stared out angrily at the world.

My mother bought me a pair of ice skates and I had lessons at the skating rink in Manchester. There was also a small riding school on the edge of Leigh and I went there to learn to ride. My mother took me to Moss Bros in Manchester and bought me expensive jodhpurs, a hacking jacket and a riding hat. I used to catch the bus from our council estate to the riding school wearing my jodhpurs and was taunted by children sniggering, 'Look at 'er ! Who does she think *she* is?' I didn't know the answer to that but I did know that one day I wanted to leave Lancashire far behind and become part of a more glamorous, self-assured world.

Occasionally, we went to the large glossy store in Manchester which was then called Kendal Milne, but I always felt we were acting the role of affluent customers and pretending to be something we weren't.

My parents were clever, original and artistically talented but they were born in an era when higher education was not a consideration for working-class families. Nevertheless, I do agree with the politician who said, 'Natural ability without education has more often raised a man to glory and virtue than education without natural ability.' When my father was a boy, he passed the scholarship and his teacher went to my granny's house to plead with her to allow him to go to the grammar school. She told him that it was utterly impossible because she was a widow. Her husband had been killed in the First World War and he died with gallantry for his country. His name is on the roll of honour on the Cenotaph in Leigh but his grateful country awarded his crippled widow just two shillings and sixpence a week to bring up two sons. Once a week, my father, as a small boy, would have to miss his school dinner and walk three miles along the canal to the colliery to collect the pitiful sum. He had to leave school as soon as it was legally possible and bring home a much-needed, if meagre, wage. We talked about it on many occasions and the memory made us both weep.

When I was growing up, I ached to live on a private estate

and so did my mother. I was an only child and she was driven by a determination to give me everything I could possibly want. Nothing was too good for me as far as she was concerned, no goal too out of reach. But the vital thing was for me to pass the scholarship. If I didn't get the scholarship, later to be called the eleven-plus, then I couldn't go to the grammar school. There would be little she could do and I would probably have to follow in her footsteps and be an assistant in the Trueform shoe shop.

For a year before the exam we talked of little else. I practised writing what we called 'stories' and we did extra sums after school. My mother had an agile mathematical brain and she could reckon up a column of figures like a computer. For months before the scholarship examination, we did mental arithmetic together. The dress I was to wear on scholarship day was washed and immaculately pressed weeks in advance. On the Friday evening before the exam, she filled the tin bath with hot water and put it in front of the fire so that I didn't have to use the tiny, freezing downstairs bathroom. On the Saturday morning, neither of us could eat but we had a cup of hot, sweet tea. 'Give it all you've got, love,' she said and there were tears in her eyes.

The scholarship exam was held in a school in the centre of Leigh and I walked there with two other girls. I was desperate to do my best and make my mother happy. She did so much for me and passing the scholarship was the one thing I could do for her. I sat down and looked at the title of the composition, which was where my greatest hopes of success rested. To this day I can remember my feelings of hopelessness when I saw the dreary, uninspiring title. 'Write a composition,' it said, 'on the difference between an apple and an orange.'

I was heartbroken and I walked home convinced I'd failed.

My mother put her arms round me and we cried in despair together. 'Never mind, love,' she said. 'I'll put the kettle on and we'll have a cup of tea,' which was her antidote to failure, heartache and desolation. Three months later we got the letter telling me that I'd passed and I think it was the happiest day of my mother's life. We both somehow knew that my world was going to change irrevocably.

The old grammar schools were not the luxury option for privileged, pampered pupils. They were the escape route for ordinary children and the pathway to a new life. My generation was the first to really leave our working-class backgrounds behind, not emotionally but in terms of opportunity. I remember the summer before I began at the grammar school as one of sheer happiness. My mother couldn't wait to take me to Danby's, the drapery shop in the centre of Leigh, to buy my uniform. On my first day at school our form teacher said, 'Hands up anyone who has a telephone?' Only one girl, Edith Greenhalgh, the daughter of a bookmaker, put up her hand and I've never envied anyone so much either before or since.

After I started at the grammar school, my father began his own painting and decorating business. He was a brilliant craftsman who did the most exquisite pine graining and his business flourished. He and my mother bought a house in a village called Culcheth, which is about five miles from Leigh, near Leigh Golf Club. Eventually, my parents became members of the club and both turned into fine golfers.

My best friend at school was the daughter of a man who worked in insurance. They lived in a big detached house. Every evening around six her mother used to change her frock before her husband came home and I was wildly impressed. Social life in our house revolved around Sunday tea, which was when visitors were invited. The meal would usually consist of tinned salmon, salad in a large glass bowl with slices of hard-boiled egg accompanied by bread and butter cut into triangles. This was followed by tinned fruit and Carnation milk, and what we called 'fancy cakes' bought from Waterfields bakery.

Although I'd very much wanted to go to the grammar school, I was never really happy there. My mother was always encouraging me to 'talk posh' with the result that I developed a false and fluctuating accent. I pronounced butter as 'batter' and, understandably, one of my end-of-term reports said, 'Lynda must try and cultivate a more natural manner.' Many years later I was doing a piece to camera for a television programme. 'Just be natural,' urged the director. 'I'm not a very natural kind of person,' I said. If ever I were left alone on a desert island, I don't know how I'd behave or speak. Even now my accent varies depending on who I'm with, which is the hallmark of the socially insecure. I'm too anxious to please and incapable of always being the same.

Despite my mother's best efforts, I remained freckled and awkward so I kept my inner yearnings to be an actress absolutely secret. If I'd expressed them, I would have been the recipient of much ridicule. When I finally told the headmistress, Miss Shanks, who was a large, athletic lady, she said, 'You can't be serious?' Undeterred, I did a lot of amateur dramatics and on stage was the only place I felt confident. At eighteen, I applied to the Guildhall School of Music and Drama in London and was awarded a place. I got on the train at Warrington Bank Quay Station with a Lancashire accent and got off at Euston without it, which meant I had to speak very slowly for a very long time.

My fellow students at drama school mostly came from

middle-class families and I kept my background to myself. I used to describe my father as a painter without adding 'and decorator'. This made things very tricky when people asked what kind of pictures he painted. 'Sort of abstract,' I said.

On one occasion, I was taken out to dinner by a posh young chap, and when he asked what I'd like as an aperitif, I was flummoxed. It was long before the days of wine bars, and finally I asked for the only drink I could think of, and said nervously, 'I'll have a port.' My escort was very sweet and said, 'I think that might be a little heavy, why not have a glass of sherry?' Thankfully, I agreed, realizing I'd made a *faux pas* but not quite knowing why. My escort never asked me out again and it was only the first of many humiliations. I used to try too hard and I was much mocked for saying to another student, 'Shall we go to the public house?' I'd been terrified that saying 'pub' might sound vulgar.

I shared a flat with a glamorous friend whose family lived in a huge house near Bristol. She took me home at weekends and I was entranced but intimidated by the English middle-class lifestyle.

While in my last term at drama school, I supported myself by working in a coffee bar in Northumberland Avenue, just by Trafalgar Square. I wrote off to various repertory companies and decided that my new stage name was to be Lynda Berrison. During my final week, I was serving behind the counter at lunchtime when the business manager from the Whitehall Theatre came in. He said, 'You're an actress, aren't you?' I said that I was and he told me they were auditioning for the juvenile lead in *Dry Rot* by John Chapman and suggested I try for it. I tore off my overall, threw on my mac over my bra and skirt and, with the manageress shouting 'Good luck', I ran across the square to the stage door of the Whitehall.

I joined a long line of pretty actresses queuing up to audition in front of Brian Rix, who ran the theatre, and actor John Slater, who was to star in the touring version of the play. When it was my turn, I walked on stage and John Slater said, 'We can't see what you look like, take your mac off.' I said, 'I can't. I'm not wearing anything underneath.' A kindly old stagehand lent me his paint-stained jersey and I auditioned for the role of middle-class Susan Wagstaff wearing that. I got the part and thought that, being an astute man of the theatre, Brian Rix recognized talent when he saw it.

Several years ago, Lord Rix wrote his autobiography and I saw to my horror how he remembered that day. 'During auditions,' he wrote, 'in walked this awkward, snub-nosed girl. She looked terrible, hair awry, over-long skirt but a croaking voice reminiscent of Glynis Johns. It was the voice that did it. Our excitement knew no bounds. We had made a discovery. "Go and get your hair done," we said. "Go and get some decent clothes. Come back at three o'clock." Our discovery duly came back, we gave her the job and she was *awful*.' At least he was then kind enough to write, 'Lynda Berrison turned into Lynda Lee-Potter, one of Fleet Street's most successful journalists. We were right about her going places, we just plumped for the wrong direction.'

We rehearsed at the Whitehall Theatre and played a week there while the resident cast had a holiday. Then we went on tour beginning at the Theatre Royal in Brighton. It was a great learning curve and a realization that social background is irrelevant in the theatre. All that matters is talent. A rather grand old actress called Cicely Walper played my mother. She said, 'Going on tour is as good as finishing school,' and in many ways she was right. I was terrible in the part but I found that I was tough enough to survive humiliation and failure, albeit frequently being anguished inside. I hid my feelings and found that pride and the ability to put on a front are effective weapons. The handsome young actor who played the male juvenile lead detested me, and whenever I blushed – which was continually – he'd say in ringing tones, 'Why has your neck gone bright red?' I knew he was deliberately trying to embarrass me and I learned another valuable lesson. The awareness that somebody wants to humiliate you decreases their power because you no longer respect them. The desire to belittle others exists in people of all social backgrounds but it's an ill-bred reaction. It's quite easy to be authoritative or the boss and give orders without demeaning people.

The class system certainly existed in theatrical digs. In my lodgings in Liverpool there were two separate sitting rooms, one for actors and one for variety performers, who were seen by landladies as a lower breed. I also saw at close quarters the ability of a star to exploit his status. One evening in Nottingham, John Slater noticed a pretty girl in the stalls. He sent someone round to invite her backstage and she remained with him until his regular girlfriend came down from London to stay with him. She, in turn, had to disappear when his wife arrived. None the less, he treated them all with great courtesy and somehow had the ability to disengage himself without degrading anyone.

Before I went on tour, I met my future husband, Jeremy, and life became complicated. He was a medical student at Guy's Hospital and lived with several other students in the flat of the eminent physician and author of medical textbooks Sir John Conybeare. I was invited there one evening for supper and Sir John, who always purported to hate women, put out a small table for my drink. I thought it was a stool so sat on it and broke it. He simply laughed and said he'd always loathed it. I am sure it wasn't true but it was a marvellous illustration of outstandingly good manners when it came to putting the feelings of a nervous guest before anything else. After that, he was always lovely to me, and when our first daughter was born, he came by tube to Dulwich Hospital clutching a bunch of roses.

Jeremy was the elder son of Air Marshal Sir Patrick Lee Potter, and when he took me home, I was scared of saying or doing the wrong thing. What I did find strange was the rigidity of meal times in his parents' house. If you arrived between meal times no refreshment of any kind would ever be offered, which was alien to the way I had been brought up. When a guest arrived at our house, my mother would say, 'I'll just put the kettle on,' whatever the time, day or night. My parents had a great friend who was a rich bookmaker and he would regularly knock on the door at about eleven o'clock in the evening on his way home from the dog track. My mother would always make tea or coffee and a pile of sandwiches and there were nights when he'd stay long after midnight.

In the Lee Potter house there were all kinds of food I'd never eaten before and meals were a nightmare. The first time we had melon, my future father-in-law handed me a bowl of ginger. I spooned it liberally over my melon as he uttered a word of caution. 'Oh I love it,' I lied, not knowing what the hell it was. Being too proud to admit that I'd overdone it, I then ate it and scalded the roof of my mouth. Two decades later I had lunch with playwright John Osborne and his wife, who served fresh figs. 'How do you eat these?' I asked and he laughed 'Oh do you remember those embarrassing years,' he said, 'when we wouldn't have had the nerve to ask?'

So-called working-class food is now considered very smart indeed. Delicacies like hotpot and spotted dick are often on

CLASS ACT

the menu at the Savoy where they are much relished by
tycoons and peers of the realm. There are tremendous
similarities between the tastes and hobbies of the aristocracy
and those of the working class, including pigeon racing, a
love of whippets and horse racing and an affection for
nursery food. The main difference is that antisocial behaviour
by the aristocracy is perceived as eccentric and in the working
classes it's seen as disgusting and vulgar. In a letter to a
friend, actress and writer Joyce Grenfell described the
experience of an acquaintance who had been to Blenheim
Palace as a guest of the late Duke and Duchess of
Marlborough for the weekend. 'The Duchess,' she wrote,
'didn't address one word to her the entire time she was there.
The Duke, who was writing letters in the library where she
was reading the paper on Sunday, got up from the desk and
went over to the fireplace where he relieved nature.'

I'm ashamed to say that I dreaded taking my new chap
home. I knew that my mother would try too hard and that I
would be embarrassed. We got engaged in London before he
actually met my parents. They were terribly pleased because
he was dazzlingly good-looking, he was going to be a doctor
and they thought he was both eligible and posh. 'I can't think
what he sees in you, love,' said my mother memorably. She
was also thrilled by my future father-in-law's title. I was
uneasy all the time because my mother behaved just as I knew
she would – over the top, forever singing my praises and desperate that her future son-in-law should like her. When she
made a delicious hotpot, he said later, 'It was like poor man's
stew.' My parents tried desperately to please him, so inevitably, and for many years, their relationship was not close.
However, after my mother died, my husband came to value
my father's emotional sweetness and clever, original brain.

16

After our engagement, my parents got a letter from my future father-in-law saying that they were pleased to welcome me into the family. But he went on to say that as his son was lucky enough to have a room in Sir John's flat, he wouldn't want him to leave until he qualified. Obviously, he said, the wedding couldn't take place for a year or so. Instantly, my fiercely proud father wrote back to say that he quite agreed. I was on my way to being a very successful actress and he certainly didn't want me getting married at this vital stage in my life.

When we finally did get married, my mother was determined to push the boat out. My uncles were instructed to wear morning suits and they hired them from Moss Bros in Manchester. My Uncle Billy was so bewitched by his own appearance that he kept posing for pictures, taken by my Aunty Elsie, before they left home and they were half an hour late arriving at church. I was tremendously impressed to discover that my male future in-laws all had their own bespoke morning suits.

My granddad was a fervent Labour supporter who despised both the medical profession and the upper classes. He was also extremely vociferous, articulate and fearless and when he'd had a drink or two he would take on anyone. Like me, my mother had a fundamentally ruthless streak. She was so determined to make sure my granddad didn't make a scene, she drugged his tea on the morning of the wedding and he slept through the entire ceremony.

My mother had organized her relations with the iron discipline of a sergeant major, with the result that my dearest aunt was so terrorized she never spoke except to say 'Yes' and to go into peals of nervous laughter when anyone asked her anything. My Aunty Susie is a brilliant, self-taught seamstress and she cut out and made my wedding dress in the front room of her house. It was the most exquisite embroidered oyster satin, bought at vast expense from Kendal Milne after my mother walked in and said, 'I want the best. I don't care what it costs.'

There were two tribes of people in the church and my in-laws were instantly recognizable as people from a different world. My mother-in-law didn't even buy a new dress. I construed this as meaning that welcoming me into the family was not the happiest day of her life and I was probably right. She never suggested what I should call her with the result that I called her Lady Lee Potter. If she'd asked me early on to call her by her Christian name, I think we might have had an easier relationship. I admire her immensely but I loved my father-in-law. He was an urbane, sophisticated man with a great knowledge and love of wine and I learned a lot from him. James Bond couldn't hold a candle to my father-in-law and, at six every evening, he made the most perfectly prepared martinis. I used to ring him up to ask him all kinds of things, and when I first bought avocados for a dinner party I said, 'Do you serve them with cream?' He explained that they weren't a pudding. He also told me I should just say avocados and not avocado pears but he always made me feel amusing rather than foolish. Again I learned that some people can tell you that you have made a social gaffe and humiliate you while others can do it in such a way that you just feel pleased that you've gained new knowledge.

All in all my wedding was a huge success because my mother ran it like an impresario putting on a West End show. There were wonderfully arranged flowers at the end of every pew and crowds flocked to the marketplace to watch the wedding guests arrive at Leigh Parish Church. I did not, of course, see my mother arrive but I'm sure she waved at everyone with the panache of a movie star. Later there were headlines in the local newspapers saying 'Actress marries Air Marshal's son,' and even a picture in *Queen* magazine. My mother was so thrilled she always kept the magazine in her handbag. She never travelled without it and would take it out when she was on the bus to show bewildered strangers. If I was with her, she'd point at me and say, 'Her father-in-law's a Sir,' and I'd want the earth to swallow me up. If only I'd had the sense to see then that she was a true life-enhancer. She wanted life to be fun, glamorous and exciting. She was so proud of me and she loved to show me off, but there was a time when I wanted her to wear Jaeger suits with a single row of pearls and look aloof. The success of my wedding gave her enormous pleasure and she never wearied of talking about it.

Marrying someone from a different social milieu brings huge problems. Both of you have to adjust, and in our case it was me who had to adjust most. I assumed that, because I was socially inferior, everything I had been brought up to do must be wrong. Of course, this was not the truth and I gradually became aware that so-called posh people can behave in a way which is vulgar. Good breeding is not the prerogative of the upper classes. I know some exceedingly grand but ghastly people. I met people who looked down on my family as social inferiors, but they were quite prepared to run up bills and make my father wait endlessly before paying him for his work. I have a vivid childhood memory of my mother sitting on the bottom of the stairs waiting for the postman in the desperate hope that an envelope containing money would arrive.

It was only when I organized my own daughter's wedding

that I realized how fantastic my mother's planning had been and in what impeccably good taste, from the stiff embossed invitations to the confetti of rose petals. She was instinctively stylish and dramatic. Also, she had a wonderful rapport with people and oh, why didn't I see it at the time? I had all the wrong values and so little sense. It's taken me a lifetime to get my priorities right. The one thing I do know is that real class is more to do with kindness and care for other people's feelings than any accident of birth.

ARE YOU A SOCIAL CLIMBER?

		Yes	No
1	At parties, are you always looking over the head of the person you're talking to in the hope of spotting someone more important?	☐	☐
2	If somebody was rude to you, would you be more likely to overlook it if they were posh?	☐	☐
3	Do you watch other people to see how to behave?	☐	☐
4	Do you automatically assume the views of those who you believe are socially superior?	☐	☐
5	Do you pretend you grew up in a much grander house than you did?	☐	☐

6 Are you ashamed of your upbringing? ☐ ☐

7 Do you talk about famous people as though
   you've met them? ☐ ☐

8 Are you having elocution lessons? ☐ ☐

9 Do you think that the way posh people
   behave socially must always be correct? ☐ ☐

10 Would you do anything to stop your boss
    meeting your parents? ☐ ☐

If you answered 'yes' to 9 or 10 of these questions, you are a
    ruthless social climber.
If you answered 'yes' to more than 5 questions, you're
    determined to be upwardly mobile.
Less than 5 and you're either not trying hard enough or you
    don't care.

2
FISH KNIVES AND SERVIETTES

Class is still an emotive word in Britain. It's considered terribly bad form to even admit there is such a thing but ask anyone what class they belong to and they will reply without a second thought. They might be wrong but they will be sure they're right. 'Does class matter?' is the vital question and, of course, it does. We'd live in a much duller world without it and we'd have no goals to strive for or attain.

The divisions between the classes might be more blurred than they were but the class system is alive and powerful. As Crestwell the butler says at the end of Noël Coward's play *Relative Values*, 'I give you a toast. I drink to the final inglorious disintegration of the most unlikely dream that ever troubled the foolish heart of man – Social Equality.' The play was written in 1950 and cheered audiences who were struggling to come to terms with Mr Attlee, a Labour government and the Festival of Britain. It was revived recently and half a century later there was nothing dated about the basic message which emphasizes the rigidity of the class structure: Joyce Grenfell talked about 'PLU' or 'People Like Us', meaning the upper class. The middle class used to say *'Pas devant la domestique'* if their husband swore in front of the daily. The lower middle class would say 'NOCD' meaning 'Not Our Class Darling' when talking about the working class.

Even now people fall into defined categories and, in fact,

25

there are more classes today than there used to be. A survey done by Essex University researchers came up with seven classes and two subclasses. They based their conclusions on the jobs we do, and leader of the research team, Professor David Rose, said, 'There is no difference on our scale between a cabinet-maker whose land-owning father went to Eton and who went to Eton himself, and a cabinet-maker whose father was an unemployed miner and went to his local comprehensive. They are both Class Five.' If this classification is accepted, then cabinet-maker Viscount Linley, who lives in a £1 million-plus house in London and has a mansion in Provence, is at the lower end of the social scale. Professor Rose and his team classify people simply by numbers, presumably on the assumption that this is the politically correct way to divide us. They ignore the fact that their classifications have nothing to do with reality. Viscount Linley is not likely to invite a Wigan chippie, son of a miner on social security, to his glamorous dinner parties. My own seven classes are the upper class, the self-made rich, the upper middle, the middle, the lower middle, the working class and the wretched scrounging class who do nothing but suck the life blood out of the country and the economy. I see no merit of any kind in them and they are costing us a fortune in benefit fraud. The other classes all have their good points and their bad, their strengths and their weaknesses.

'I want to see a classless society,' said Tony Blair when he became Prime Minister. John Major said the same thing during his leadership, and in his egalitarian quest he abolished evening dress for a Party Conference ball in Blackpool. This was an enormous mistake as Party members want to feel part of the élite not *hoi polloi*. You don't join the Tory Party because you want to be part of the common herd.

You join it because you wish to be upwardly mobile and a cut above everyone else. John Major was very touchy about class insults. He cared obsessively what was written about him in the press and a critical comment could ruin his day. Douglas Hurd used to try and hide the London *Evening Standard* from him but he could ferret it out with unerring instinct. He would then pore over it and analyse every word. The ability to be insulted is said to be in inverse ratio to intelligence. Undeniably, it's also in inverse ratio to social background. Margaret Thatcher pretended to ignore her violent critics and used to say to colleagues, 'I never listen to the *Today* programme. It's so hostile. It was particularly bad this morning.'

The expressed desire to abolish the class system is meant to demonstrate that the speaker is a lovely, unspoilt person who regards everyone as equal, and the premise is, quite frankly, absurd. The only people who hanker after a classless society are those who want what other people have without working for it. We are not all equal or prepared to put in the same amount of effort, so we don't deserve the same rewards.

When Barbara Cartland was interviewed by a northern radio reporter, he said, 'Tell me, Dame Barbara, do you think we now have a classless society?' 'Of course we have,' she said, 'or I wouldn't be sitting here talking to somebody like *you*.' Dame Barbara also said, when David Beckham and his wife Victoria, otherwise known as Posh Spice, bought a vast house near her own over-furnished mansion, 'We don't want people like that moving here and bringing down the neighbourhood,' which was an ill-bred remark but then there was something inherently vulgar about Dame Barbara, with her shocking-pink frocks matching her shocking-pink rouge. Her servants were terrified of her, which is understandable as she was autocratic and overpowering. Actually, she was a monster and a snob who despised the *nouveaux riches*.

Nouveaux riches have thick white carpets and vast Jacuzzis in their 'His and Hers' bathrooms. The self-made millionaire has little time for the poor. He thinks they should be kept in their place, which is the council estate *he* has climbed out of. He has absolutely no desire to do anything for charity unless he thinks it might get him a knighthood. Unlike the old-fashioned aristocrat, he does not want to do good works by stealth. He wants any generosity on his part to be trumpeted from the rooftops. His natural response to any request for help is 'What's in it for me?' He's very partial to beige trousers with razor-sharp creases and blazers with gold buttons and he likes to be weighed down with gold jewellery. He has a permanent tan the colour of boot polish and bears a startling resemblance to Jimmy Tarbuck. He likes to give swimming parties to show off his new pool and his body now that he's got his own personal trainer. Most *nouveaux* are misogynists and don't think girls should be over-educated because 'it gives them ideas', meaning 'the ridiculous idea that they are as good as men'. They are so touchy about their age that they often dump their first wife when they spot her first stretch mark. They then buy her a house in Marbella and marry somebody younger. They rarely marry socially upwards because they like to feel superior to the women in their lives.

There is an essential desire in most of us to prosper, learn and succeed. I don't believe that we ought to be satisfied with our lot. If you are Earl Spencer, of course, and own Althorp, then fair enough, but I've always wanted something bigger and better. When we first moved into our current house, we had six acres, which I thought was half of England. We were invited to a local party and a fellow guest said, 'Have you got much land?' I said, 'Gosh yes, we've got six acres. How much have you got?' 'Thirty thousand,' he replied. We now have ten acres, but land makes you acquisitive so I long for twenty. Personally, I think you can't be too thin, too rich, live in too big a house or have too much land. When the grandson of a *Daily Mirror* printer won a scholarship to Eton, he described a school friend to his mother and said, 'His back garden is Essex.' I don't know what happened to the landowner's son, but the printer's Etonian grandson became head boy.

There was a period when the social structure in Britain was so rigid it was almost impossible to move from one class into another unless you were stunningly attractive or a genius. Indeed the aristocracy has been enriched by being infiltrated by more than one dynamic beauty from the variety theatre. Interestingly, at university most students make friends in their very first week with undergraduates from identical backgrounds who went to the same kind of schools and have parents in similar professions. There is surprisingly little mobility so what does this prove? First of all, that most of us are happier and feel safer with people who have the same behavioural patterns. If there is any mobility, then infiltrating outsiders take on the mores of the group.

The way we eat is vital in a relationship and romances can break up over the way somebody holds a fork or knife, particularly if they hold it like a pencil. In his autobiography, actor Martin Jarvis describes how Susan Hampshire, who played opposite him in the television series *The Forsyte Saga*, pointed out to him that he was holding his knife in an incorrect way. Martin grew up in South London and went to school in Croydon. 'My suburban slip,' he writes, 'was showing.' It's over thirty years ago, but obviously the incident still rankles.

The late playwright Dennis Potter was interviewed on television when he was at New College, Oxford. He was the son of a Gloucestershire miner in the days when few working-class boys went to university, let alone Oxford. Most of his new university friends had been to Eton or Winchester. They were all clever and so was he, but he said that when his working-class girlfriend came from his home village to see him, she was miserable and his friends were ill at ease. The truth was, I imagine, that he was the one who was ill at ease. I know how he felt because there was a time when I felt I straddled two worlds and was uneasy in both of them. When you are becoming upwardly mobile, there can be a false tendency to think that everything in the new world is beyond criticism. Initially, the mistake upstarts like me make is in believing that the world we are leaving behind is inferior in every way to the world we are entering.

Aristocrats and the upper classes are so confident that they never have doubts about being boring or unfanciable. The prospect of a title through marriage is so appealing that many an ambitious, upwardly mobile girl has succumbed. The reason a lot of them turn into Lady Bountifuls is because they can't stand being *à deux* with their husband. They are sexually unfulfilled and bounding with energy so they spend their time doing good works in the community, organizing charity fairs, balls and political fund-raising events.

Too much of this can cause trouble as Lady Cobham demonstrated after she met the former Secretary of State for Heritage David Mellor. She ran off with him and gave up Hagley Hall, which is a 100-roomed mansion in 1,500 acres. However, it is slightly shabby, on the edge of suburbia, not a million miles from Birmingham and has to be run as a conference centre to earn enough money to maintain it. Lady Cobham and Mr Mellor consummated the affair in Viscount Cobham's own bed at his London flat, which is a frightfully lower-middle-class thing to do. 'Mellor is a dog,' thundered the Viscount. 'He came to stay here but do a dog a favour and it bites you. Virtue, honour, loyalty just don't seem to be part of his makeup. He and his like live in a *demi-monde* believing they are the movers and shakers and failing to recognize that they are not. They are little people who think they are big.' Certainly, the poet Richard Lovelace's philosophy of 'I could not love thee (Dear) so much, Lov'd I not honour more' is not part of David Mellor's lower-middle-class Dorset background.

Undeniably, there is an aristocratic shape and most aristocrats are tall and lean. The upper-class playwright Nell Dunn said that if people were naked, it would be impossible to guess their class. But I agree with Glenda Jackson who comes from a working-class family and says that a naked working-class body would be instantly recognizable on account of it being short and sturdy with a low bottom and knobbly feet.

Elderly upper-class ladies are still to be found in crumbling Scottish castles or living in private hotels in South Kensington or Cheltenham. Often they are secretaries of their local Conservative Party where they terrorize the sitting Member. Real ladies never talk about their background. They do not say, 'I'm beerage not peerage,' as did one rather vulgar honourable, who inherited her fortune from a Scottish brewery. They assume that everyone always knows who they are. 'Hello is that you? It's me,' Lady Astor would say on the telephone to her butler Lee, the King or a peer of the realm. And, as Lady Aldington, who is the niece of the great Lord Curzon, said to me, 'I'm Old Testament, black or white, blood and thunder, right or wrong. My husband is much more Christian. He's New Testament. He says you have to look at the other person's side. But I think that takes up too much time.'

Upper-class women disregard all physical ailments and think being ill is more shaming than bankruptcy. They dismiss chronic influenza as 'nothing the matter', double pneumonia as 'a slight chill' and are astride a horse three days after childbirth. They are energetic, continually forcing everyone out on five-mile hikes in all weathers. In later life, they acquire the complexion of a deep-sea fisherman with a taste for the bottle. They can be very mean and extremely economical, forever unpicking string. They shamelessly dump any present you give them that they don't like into a drawer and later give it to their cook or the gardener's wife when she has a baby. When my second daughter was born, my mother-in-law gave me some eau-de-Cologne in a faded box which, without a doubt, had been in her escritoire for many a long year. Ladies, unlike *arrivistes* like me, are appalled, not pleased, by extravagant presents. When Princess Diana spent her first royal Christmas at Sandringham, she bought expensive, glamorous things for everyone, only to find that this was frowned upon. The royal family prefer jokey or practical presents and, apparently, one year the Queen was enchanted by a mop on a stick for washing up after barbecues.

Ladies regularly cook, sew, garden and ride to hounds with the cut-throat professionalism of world-beaters. They then dismiss their expertise with a light laugh as something anyone could do, given five minutes' instruction and a handbook. 'I'm not a professional writer,' said Lady Soames modestly when she wrote a brilliant biography of her mother, Lady Churchill. She produced 556 pages, never having written more than a shopping list before.

Ladies are marvellous at getting rid of you without ever actually suggesting you go. I interviewed a countess and suddenly found myself on the drive saying goodbye long before I had planned to leave. They are also terribly good at giving orders to their staff, unlike women who have married above their station and find it almost impossible. I'm incapable of telling anyone to do anything and precede any request with flowery, anxious-to-please phrases.

Ladies have full control over their facial reactions. The muscles of one of my in-laws didn't even flicker as her daily absent-mindedly blew her nose on the drying-up cloth. Ladies can be scruffy without looking sluttish and never keep their new frock for best or wear bedroom slippers. Upper-class Shirley Williams, at the height of her political powers, always looked as though she'd just scrambled through a prickly hedge, which was not a look the lower-middle-class Lady Thatcher could ever have carried off. Ladies are incredibly rude and can squash you with an inconsequence. 'Jessie thought the orchestra rails were beautifully polished,' said Lady Bull after she went with her maid to watch her actor son, Peter, in *Waiting for Godot* and he was unwise enough to ask her what she thought of his performance.

Years ago, I went to interview Lady Bathurst and she said crushingly, 'I knew you were a journalist as soon as you telephoned and pronounced my name with a long A when it should be a short one.' I felt rather bitter as it had taken me over twenty years to learn to rhyme bath with path and not maths. The pronunciation of upper-class names is a minefield, especially when you have people such as the

eminent writer Anthony Powell, whose surname is pronounced Pole. I once said it correctly to Jilly Cooper's
husband Leo and I saw a look of amazement flash across his
face. Clearly, he had previously judged me to be a peasant.

The upper classes seldom reveal their feelings and it's
impossible to tell from their faces whether they are ecstatic,
heartbroken or triumphant. A lady is never embarrassed and
has a unique phraseology that no one else would have the
nerve to use. 'We divided them into flirts, certs and wayside
pleasures,' one old lady said on television as she reminisced
about the beaux who had courted her at débutante dances.
Meanwhile, the pecking order remains and even débutantes
still exist. The prettiest are to be found every year modelling
high fashion at the Berkeley Dress Show, which in the year
2000 took place for the forty-eighth time in aid of the NSPCC.
Lady Isabella Hervey, sister of the Marquess of Bristol, was
one of the models and her mother, Yvonne Marchioness of
Bristol, said, 'She is hoping to follow in her sister Victoria's
footsteps by becoming an international model. I'm sure she
will be a huge success.' If a lower-middle or working-class
mother had said this, there would have been much sneering
laughter but aristocrats get away with being big-headed.

There is nothing prudish about the upper classes and they
never either complain or explain. When the painter Lord
Aberdeen wrote a letter to a newspaper talking fondly about
the brothels of his youth, he became known in his family as
the Brothel Marquis. Evidently, such establishments were
used by rich and aristocratic clients and flourished in the
forties and fifties. There was Mrs Fetherstonehaugh's private
hotel in Kensington and a brothel in Paris run by Vicomtesse
de Brissac. 'It was all very jolly,' said Lady Aberdeen. 'Gosh
there's no prudery and primness in our family. We laugh at

these things. When a young journalist rang me up from the *Evening Standard*, I said to her, 'I don't want you to think I was one of those luscious ladies from Mrs Fetherstonehaugh's establishment, because I'm sorry to say I wasn't.' The modern version of Mrs Fetherstonehaugh's brothel is the massage parlour which, despite bad publicity, continues to exist.

Most upper-class women relish being battleaxes, and when Lady Aberdeen's daughter told her that people are terrified of her, she said, 'Hurrah. Awfully good news.' They have an obsessive need to win, like Princess Anne who is an aggressive woman with the killer instinct. Luckily, her son and daughter are equally competitive. If they'd been shy and backward, she would have had little sympathy and insisted they buck their ideas up. She's always wanted to make her children tough, not cosseted. When she was young, she would make Princes Charles cry because she thought he was soppy. Upper-class women are fundamentally much more strident and steelier than their male counterparts. If a lady is also rich, she's often terrifying and a *monstre sacré*.

Real ladies think emotion is a rather nasty modern habit. 'The very idea that children want to be cuddled by a complete stranger I find utterly amazing,' Princess Anne remarked tartly. Many dukes have socially inferior mistresses because the only affection they were ever shown as children was from their lower-middle-class nanny.

Travel writer and *bon viveur* the late Quentin Crewe was the grandson of the Marquess of Crewe. His mother, Lady Annabel Crewe, was a crashing snob. Her second husband was a brilliant horseman and the most elegant fencer in Britain. He was handsome and brave but shamingly middle class. 'I had never seen fish knives until I married your father,' Lady Annabel once said to Quentin.

No doubt she'd never seen napkin rings either. The lower classes didn't use napkins, the upper classes had new napkins every day and only the middle classes put their used ones into silver rings. There is still a club in Leeds where members have individual pigeonholes for their napkin rings. The lower middle class mainly used patterned paper ones and called them serviettes. John Betjeman lampooned them in his famous verse 'How to Get On in Society':

Phone for the fish-knives, Norman,
As Cook is a little unnerved;
You kiddies have crumpled the serviettes
And I must have things daintily served.

The lower middle classes desperately want to be dainty and ladylike, which they think means being ultra-refined, and they have a great love of what they call knick-knacks.

Quentin Crewe's aunt was as snobbish as his mother, and when served with an egg mousse for dinner, said pointedly, 'How amusing to have a luncheon dish at dinner.' After Lady Annabel's son, Shane, was killed fighting in Italy in 1943, she merely said it was a pity he'd had all his teeth out in a painful operation before he died, as it seemed such a waste. Then she never spoke of his death again. When she was told by an eminent physician that Quentin, who had muscular dystrophy, would die before he was sixteen, she refused to discuss the matter and ignored his disability. There was no weeping or even any concession to her son's frailty. The result was that he became tough, resilient, physically fearless and treated his illness as a bore, not a handicap. He also proved the physician wrong and survived until his late sixties. There is something noble about the stoicism of the upper classes.

After Lord Uxbridge had his leg shot off at the Battle of Waterloo, the Duke of Wellington said, 'By God, Uxbridge, you've lost your leg.' Lord Uxbridge looked down and said, 'By God, sir, so I have.' And nothing further was said on the subject.

Like many men from his background, Quentin Crewe was laid back about infidelity. 'It can be a shock when one's wife is unfaithful,' he said, 'but not to the point of making too much of it.' Middle-class husbands mind much more because they lack the confident arrogance of the upper class and take infidelity personally. They assume it must be their fault for being inadequate lovers whereas the upper classes never blame themselves for anything. Also, they know that some women are constitutionally unfaithful because they crave admiration more than lust.

Graham Greene based his famous novel *The End of the Affair* on his long sexual liaison with the married Catherine Walston. Her husband, Lord Walston, accepted the affair with equanimity. When his wife and her lover went to stay at Villa Rosaio, the novelist's house on Capri, he wrote to her saying that he hoped they were having a good time. Equally, Catherine was not jealous of Graham Greene's other mistresses, including artist Jocelyn Rickards. This irritated the novelist, who would say accusingly, 'If you aren't jealous you don't love me,' which was rather bourgeois. When Catherine died in 1978, Lord Walston wrote a consoling letter to Graham Greene, saying that his wife had been taught many things by her lover, and one of them was joy.

Quentin Crewe was an expert on the ruthlessness of upper-class women as his first great love was Lady Dorothy Macmillan's daughter Sarah. The beautiful, headstrong Sarah was actually the offspring of Lady Dorothy's lover, Lord

Boothby, although Lady Dorothy remained with her husband, Harold Macmillan, until the end of her life. When Sarah became pregnant, her domineering mother decided that the scandal would harm Macmillan's political career and forced her to have an abortion. 'I don't know if it was my child,' Quentin Crewe said in an interview before his death, 'but it was awful because the abortion made it impossible for her to conceive again.' Sadly, Sarah sought solace in drugs and drink and died at thirty-nine, having become an alcoholic. Lady Dorothy never showed by word or deed that she felt either guilt or remorse.

One of the great strengths of the upper classes is that they never worry about what other people think or say about them. It doesn't occur to them to care because they are sure that their way of doing things is the correct way and they are utterly indifferent to scandal. The downside of this is that they can be cruel and hurt the feelings of a lot of people. If they have sensitive children, then they can sometimes make harsh and unfeeling parents. Unlike the middle classes, they do not have a desperate interest in education for their daughters. Fathers often send their sons to Eton or Harrow because it's where they went themselves. Their daughters rarely go to university, although some of them still go to fantastically expensive finishing schools in Switzerland, as did the young Diana Spencer. When they return home, Daddy buys them a flat, usually in a Kensington mansion block. I would be amazed if Princesses Beatrice and Eugenie go to university.

The upper class feel an affinity with the working class but despise the middle class as jumped-up and a bit pretentious. When Ian Fleming and his wife Ann moved briefly to Canterbury in the late fifties, she wrote in a letter to Evelyn

Waugh, 'We have to entertain or be entertained by the neighbours, they fall into that category of person which is ever increasing, and neither "landed" nor "peasantry". The doctor's wife gave a cocktail party for us in a low-rafted room.' It seems that a doctor's wife was perceived as middle class and beyond the pale. The working class, on the other hand, think doctors are posh.

When comedian Bernard Manning's late wife asked me what my husband did and I said he was a doctor, she said admiringly, 'You have done well for yourself, haven't you?'

The RAF, unlike the army, has always looked benevolently on eccentric spouses. There was an air vice-marshal at RAF Halton in Buckinghamshire who used to have a picture of his naked wife in her younger days in a silver frame on the grand piano. And when I was an RAF wife living in Aden, the CO's wife's party trick was to wear a reversible dress. She was a heavy drinker who wore it one side during the soup and the entrée and changed it to the other side between the pudding and the cheese. The guests were usually junior in rank to the host, so no one ever commented. Wives were always afforded the title of their husband and I was known as Mrs Squadron Leader Lee-Potter. At one RAF station, I met an old friend, an actress who was married to a corporal. We hugged each other and I was told by the CO's wife it was unseemly to behave in such a friendly way to the wife of an airman.

There are those who ache to be middle class and those who see it as a ghastly and shaming state. When movie star Hugh Grant began doing interviews, his mother, who has rather posh ancestors, gave her famous son two bits of advice. 'Don't say pubic hair, darling,' she said, 'because it's not funny. And please don't keep saying we're middle class.' However, Sir John Mortimer has defended middle-class values and admires their virtues of tolerance and liberalism. 'The middle classes,' he says, 'have been the source of most of the strength of England and most writers have come from the middle class. With the exception of Byron and Shelley, the aristocracy hasn't produced many writers and working-class traditions have tended to keep people in rather stereotyped conditions of mind. Political change also has come mainly from the middle classes.'

Sir John is upper middle class and, despite tolerance and liberalism, the upper middles and middles are very different groups. On the whole, they wouldn't dream of mixing socially but both groups are obsessive about education. Daughters of mill owners were some of the first women to go to college. Some parents, particularly the women, have come from the working class and made the switch when they went from grammar school to university. They may be lawyers, filmmakers, accountants or consultants and worry endlessly about their children not being clever. They are highly competitive and go to the gym or have personal trainers to get them fit enough to win the parents' race on sports day. Mummies are divided into those who have their own careers and those who turn being a wife and perfect hostess into an art form. They start visiting nursery and prep schools before they give birth. On their child's first day at prep school they say, 'We must organize a mummies' lunch.' If they live in London, they would die rather than send Christian or Felicity to a state school. Some of them vote Labour and would deny being snobs, but the first question they ask when their child mentions a school friend is, 'What do his mummy and daddy do?'

The ones who haven't married above their station went to famous girls' schools like Wycombe Abbey, Cranborne

Chase or Wentworth, where they learned loyalty and the need to contribute, play the game and develop an ability to always look on the bright side. They live in Georgian terraces or old farmhouses and, at the top end of the scale, have a few pieces of good furniture inherited from their parents. Unlike the upper class, they are committed to the schools where their children are educated and are totally involved in all projects from fund-raising to drama productions. High-powered mummies with demanding jobs get up at 6 a.m. in order to have what they call 'quality time' with their children, which involves forcing them to do extra sums. Many of them rely on a northern nanny and live in fear of her teaching her charges to say 'pardon', 'lounge' or 'toilet'. Their kitchens are usually massive with paintings done by their children on the wall, a vast table, the smell of real coffee and a giant dresser bedecked with Emma Bridgewater mugs. Agas remain popular, although the farmhouse-style kitchen is now slightly *passé*, and there is much more steel and chrome and limestone floors than stripped pine. Television broadcaster and columnist Anne Robinson even has limestone floors in her hall but then she also has an indoor swimming pool.

Upper-middle-class mummies have little trouble with au pairs because they are naturally authoritative and so lay down strict rules right at the beginning. A mummy who was once working class will grit her teeth when the au pair uses her expensive scent, stays out late, flirts with Daddy or cooks for herself and fails to wash up. After three months, the resentment finally bursts open and she screams her head off over something unbelievably trivial. The au pair then takes umbrage and has to be shunted off to one of the convents which gives shelter to fallen au pairs.

The strength of the upper middle classes is their work-horse mentality, their perfectionism and their touching belief that they can juggle fifteen balls in the air without dropping any. On Saturdays, they take the children for swimming and riding lessons. When they go to gymkhanas, they cheer their offspring with all the fervour of Alex Ferguson urging on Manchester United. Names like Tamsin and Tarquin have had their day and Bert and Alf, which used to be the prerogative of the aristocracy and the working class, are becoming increasingly popular.

The middle classes really came into being with the advent of mill owners and newly rich capitalists during the industrial revolution in the nineteenth century. The middle classes, as opposed to the upper middle, frequently live in mock-Tudor estates. They are very hot on neighbourhood watch schemes and reach positions of giddy authority in parent–teacher associations. They are heavily into joining in and contributing to the community. They belong to the Lions and Rotary and become captains of golf clubs. They are self-made so they think their children ought to be equally capable. They do not mollycoddle their sons and daughters and are quite happy for them to do paper rounds. Wives have a regular weekly appointment at the local hairdressing salon and tell their gay hairdresser that their husband would kill them if they had their hair cut. They are keen on stockings and suspenders and think it's important to keep romance in their marriage so they leave the children with their parents and go for weekends to the smarter Spanish resorts.

People are usually proud of their working-class or upper-class backgrounds but nobody ever brags about being lower middle class. Novelist Adele Parks says, 'I'm from that rarely talked-about breed, the lower middle class, too poor to be posh, too posh to be patronized.' Gentility is their religion, they yearn to be refined and they are terrified of being thought common. They keep their most expensive clothes for what they call 'best' and put embroidered covers on the arms and backs of chairs to stop them getting grubby. The women wear high heels with trousers and walk like Dick Emery. They look down on the working class, and call their husband 'Daddy'. In restaurants, they talk in whispers and try and eat crisps quietly. Politician Mo Mowlam comes from a similar background but rebelled and was famed in the House of Commons in her younger days for her fund of *risqué* stories

No doubt Mrs Betty Kenwood, the retired social diarist of the now defunct *Queen* magazine, had the lower middles in mind when she wrote, 'We stayed in such a tranquil hotel and fortunately one didn't see any of those ghastly coach tour people that one occasionally comes across when one is abroad.' One, of course, is the operative word, as Princess Anne has proved more than twice.

The middle classes are not as possessive as the working classes and do not say, 'my dad', 'my aunty' or 'my best friend'. Neither do they proffer invitations by saying, 'Come for your tea.' After all, you're not going to go for anyone else's tea.

A working-class wife fries breakfast in her quilted dressing gown, wearing the bedroom slippers she always wears indoors. In the evening, after rushing in from work, she starts cooking while still wearing her coat, having been brainwashed all her life into believing that her husband must have his dinner on the table the minute he gets home. The middle-class husband is quite prepared to wait, have a drink or even bath the baby. Middle-class wives think it's important that fathers bond with their children. On the whole, working-class husbands, in common with upper-class fathers, do not help with babies. As one Tottenham footballer said, 'I do the decorating but the baby's hers.' The middle-class husband will be prepared to worry about nebulous things like his wife's state of mind, her intellectual stimulation and whether or not she feels emotionally fulfilled. The working-class husband's idea of being good to his wife is to agree to babysit while she goes to watch a male stripper in the local pub.

When I was a child, most working-class men did hard labouring jobs in the pit or the factories, so when they got home they were physically weary and expected a hot meal to be waiting on the table. Before I got married, the only advice my mother gave me was that I must always have the table laid for dinner when my husband got home and I don't remember either my granddad or my father ever doing any kind of domestic chore.

During the early part of the twentieth century, the workers became more prosperous and therefore more upwardly mobile. A Latvian Jewish tailor, called Montague Burton, spotted a gap in the market and in 1904 opened his first made-to-measure Burtons in Chesterfield. Money was so tight he slept in the shop at night. By 1910 he had four shops, and in 1921 he opened the first Burtons in Leeds. Until then, working-class men had rarely owned a suit and Montague filled a need with the slogan 'A suit for every working man'. The demand was so gigantic that on Saturday mornings the queues would stretch around the block and staff used to come out with chairs and trays of tea. Burton was one of the first employers to treat workers with respect and there was a resident doctor, dentist, chiropodist and a canteen which could seat 8,000 at one sitting. Each morning and afternoon cake trolleys were wheeled around when the workers took a break. At about the same time, Yates's wine lodges were opening and again expanding the world of the working class. Young couples could toast their engagement with the draught champagne Yates's were famed for. Respectable women who wouldn't be seen in pubs could go to the wine lodges and buy the most popular drink which was white wine and hot lemon and called an 'All In'. It was the earliest beginning of a conviction that you could be working class and upwardly mobile and have some of the good things in life.

It was also the start of working-class confidence but not the end of class awareness which is as fundamental to human beings as lust and greed. As one wise social commentator said crisply, 'The desire for social equality is based on an ancient and inaccurate assumption that, as we are all equal in the eyes of God, we should be equally equal in the eyes of our fellow men. The fact that it doesn't work out like that and never will, in no way deters the idealists from working towards that Utopia where we are all hail fellow well met and there is no waiting at table.'

Actor Tom Courtenay, who was born in Hessle Road near the Hull dockyards where his father painted trawlers, believes that what he calls 'the superior working class' is a vanished breed. 'People like my parents,' he says, 'don't exist any more. There's no work, no community left. They've all gone to live on those horrible housing estates. Hessle Road has disappeared, all the houses demolished. People were more decent then. There was no crime on Hessle Road although people were poor.'

The scrounging class of course is a subspecies who bear absolutely no resemblance to the proud, indomitable working class which respected authority and believed in education.

Our welfare system was introduced to give the vulnerable a helping hand in desperate times. However, social security fraud now costs us £4 billion a year. It is seen by the scroungers as a bottomless money pot into which they continually dip to fund the capitalist lifestyle they think they deserve. One benefit cheat was eventually sent to prison for claiming money for forty-three children and housing benefit for eleven fictitious residences over fourteen years.

The scroungers have no need of social skills because they have no one to impress and no wish to anyway. All they want is what they see as their rights and they are adept at milking the system. Meanwhile, their children exist in grim homes where they are more likely to get a slap than a cuddle. The only male presence comes from a series of boyfriends who stay long enough to be violent and then disappear. The siblings have different fathers. They live on chips and in the summer their scraggy bodies get even frailer because they don't have the luxury of school dinners. Magazines read by children as young as nine years old dish out a diet of soft porn and describe sexual positions in explicit detail. These children don't live in a poverty trap but their jobless parents put their own appetites first. Their homes don't lack the material things of life, as the scrounging class are expert at extracting every penny of social security they can get. They have cars, stereos, videos and enough money to drink themselves senseless. They earn none of it so they don't respect their possessions or themselves. Everyone looks down on them but they don't care. If any teacher has the temerity to criticize the behaviour of their child, they clout the teacher.

ARE YOU POSH?

	Yes	No
1 Do you live in a house that's been in your family for generations?	☐	☐
2 Was your mother a deb?	☐	☐
3 Have you got a family motto?	☐	☐
4 Do you assume that everyone goes to Ascot, Glyndebourne, Henley and Cowes?	☐	☐
5 Are you a trust-fund child?	☐	☐
6 Do you have your own shoot?	☐	☐
7 If somebody invites you to play tennis, do you assume it will be on their own court?	☐	☐
8 Do you have land rather than merely a garden?	☐	☐
9 Do you call your grandfather 'Grandpapa'?	☐	☐
10 Do you stay with Lord and Lady Vestey for the Cheltenham Jumping Festival?	☐	☐

If you answered 'yes' to 7–10 of these questions, you're
   extremely posh.
If you answered 'yes' to more than 3 questions, you're pretty
   top drawer.
If you answered 'no' to every question, you'll just have
   to keep on doing the lottery.

3
SNOBS AND SNEERS

Like class, snobbery will always be with us. The over-whelming success of the television series *Keeping Up Appearances* was due to the fact that many of us recognized aspects of the snobbish Hyacinth in ourselves. We saw in her our desire to move onwards and upwards and to improve our standing in the eyes of others. Snobbery usually means we want to make ourselves sound more important and knowledgeable, which is a natural human instinct. We want to move to a better address and drink something better than Asti spumante, which I once thought was the smartest drink in the world. I even used to drink gin and orange which is about as naff as you can get. I'd die of thirst now or turn teetotal rather than touch gin and orange. I had my last one on the day I read in *Vogue* that it was the favourite drink of the wives of junior RAF officers. Although we laughed at Hyacinth, it was with great affection and occasionally anguish when she did something particularly crass. She was dreadful but she was also vulnerable.

Hyacinth would have been in ecstasy if she had ever met Lady Celestria Noel who is the former social editor of *Harpers & Queen*. Lady Celestria epitomizes everything Hyacinth craved and has given gloriously grand advice about how to cope with the Season:

If you are attending many events, it is sensible to prepare

for the fray. This means not only organizing your Ascot outfit in good time, but also a visit to a health farm in late March or April. Plan any major hair and beauty projects ahead so that you are as thin and brown as possible before having to don summer clothes, which are far less forgiving than winter woollies. When I was attending almost all the Season's events, I would try to get some winter sun in March after Cheltenham and before the Berkeley Dress Show to give me a boost.

The words were written in the year 2000 but sound as though they were composed in the 1930s when ladies would never go out without a hat and came home to find their maid laying out their evening clothes. Lady Celestria tries to explain how egalitarian the Season is and says:

Among the many fallacies about the Season is that it is exclusively for the very rich. I want to show that it is one of the best forms of entertainment England has to offer and that people should shelve their prejudices and get out there and enjoy it. It really is good value for money. Ascot is only about £60 per ticket per day. I think it is a shame that inverted snobbery causes so few people who could be enjoying it to take part in it.

She explains that neither need we worry about clothes. 'All the clever older women like my mother,' she says, 'have village dressmakers who simply copy their good clothes of old.' I haven't laughed so much since the teenage Prince Charles went up to a working-class little Welsh girl, pointed to her granny and said, 'Is she your Nanny?'

There is an element of snobbery in most of us but on the

whole we deny this integral part of human nature. At least royal couturier Hardy Amies has the courage to be honest. He's a self-confessed snob who says that if he has to be bored at parties he prefers to be bored by the grand and is not over-fond of the class of people he describes as 'rather *nouveau*'. This is a phrase used by the late great snob Nicholas Ridley. When he was Secretary of State for the Environment he outraged owners of historic buildings by saying that if the *anciens pauvres* hadn't enough money to look after their houses, 'the *nouveaux riches* would just have to move in.' Move in they did and many historic houses are now owned by pop stars.

A few years ago Norton Radstock town council in Avon wanted to change the name of a private housing estate from Wellow Brook Meadow to Reg Jones Close. Dear old Reg was a miner, the salt of the earth and proudly working class. When residents objected to the change in name and, as they saw it, status, a local councillor said, 'This is people's snobbery coming out, I'm afraid.' Of course it was, but what's wrong with that? Reg Jones Close sounds remarkably like a council estate, and if you've progressed enough to be able to buy your own house, you want the address to make that quite clear. The upwardly mobile do not live in closes or cul-de-sacs.

Snobbery is a powerful drive in most people who have progressed from humble beginnings. It has certainly motivated me all my life. I may be ridiculous but I don't care. At a fête I was opening, I was presented with a lavatory-roll holder which was disguised as a crinoline doll. It was horrendous but as I was staying with a friend that weekend I gave it to her as a joke. The next time I stayed I was appalled to see that the doll was in her bathroom with a note pinned to it saying 'Lynda Lee-Potter gave me this'.

Royalty has thrown up quite a few snobs, including King Edward VII, who was extremely snobbish about dress. When an admiral's daughter attended a party wearing a frock that was above her ankles he snorted, 'I'm afraid you must have made a mistake. This is a dinner not a tennis party.' And when he saw Lord Harris at Ascot in a tweed suit he said, 'Goin' ratting, Harris?'

Had Queen Mary been lower middle class and not royal, she would have been called a freeloader. If she looked at an *objet d'art* in anyone's mansion and said, 'I like that,' what she really meant was, 'I'll have it,' and invariably it was handed over.

Tory MP Michael Jopling famously sneered at Michael Heseltine as being a bit of a *nouveau* because he'd had to buy his own furniture. Alan Clark said he thought this was rather a snobbish remark, although he was not devoid of snobbishness himself. His wife Jane condemned two of his mistresses who sold their story to the *News of the World* by saying, 'If you bed people of below-stairs class they will go to the newspapers.' One of Britain's greatest snobs is Nicholas Van Hoogstraten, the property tycoon. He's building a £30m Renaissance-style palace on his High Cross Estate in East Sussex. He sees himself as the last representative of a belligerent British Empire and has claimed that the only purpose of creating wealth is to separate oneself from the riff-raff. He's had frequent battles with the Ramblers Association, and on Radio 4's *Today* programme said, 'I'm not having anyone on my land. They will never get away with it. I have been picked on by these disgusting people who have nothing better to do.' He sounds ghastly but at least he has the courage to be honest.

I'm not totally without sympathy, as I couldn't stand any

strangers striding across my land. The Ramblers are an aggressive lot who have thousands of miles in which to roam, so I don't think they do too badly. Country lovers do not all have gentle, easy-going natures as they seem to be permanently engaged in battle. Rather than being grateful to the landowners who do let them walk across fields, they bitterly resent anyone who doesn't want to give them complete open access.

Interestingly, it is the aristocracy on the whole who are co-operative and the newly rich who are fiercely possessive about land. When pop star Gary Barlow bought Delamere Manor with its 60-acre estate in Cheshire, he immediately stopped the local anglers from fishing in his lake as they had done for generations. And I don't blame him.

When I suggested in the *Daily Mail* that we all ought to offer accommodation to Kosovan refugees, one irate reader wrote to say, 'Let Lynda Lee-Potter put the refugees on the ten acres she's so proud of.' I rather envy Mrs Steve Ovett who told me that they had lived in their mansion on the Scottish borders for weeks before they discovered that there was an entire wing they hadn't realized existed. Fiona Fullerton brags that, in her stately Gloucestershire house, she has six lavatories, which is very smart. She also says that if you have a picture of yourself shaking hands with a famous politician, or a Christmas card from the Queen, then it's naff to display it in the drawing room but OK to show it off in the downstairs lavatory. I'm not so sure but it's definitely naff to have any invitation from a duke or a royal on the mantelpiece six months after the party. I have rude or entertaining letters on my downstairs lavatory walls. These include one from Lord Snowdon pointing out an error I made in my interview with him. 'Dear Lynda Lee-Potter,' he wrote, 'I wasn't called

Fishpaste at school I was called Fishcake.' There is also one from Denis Thatcher which says, 'The answer to your ever charming request for an interview is of course, "No".' I was once introduced as 'That famous household name everybody knows and loves . . . Belinda Line Porter.' So I've never had the chance to get above myself. But I can well understand why Beryl Mooney changed her name to Bel, which is a far more suitable name for Mrs Jonathan Dimbleby. I just wish I'd had the same foresight, instead of sticking with a name which is not a million miles removed from Sharon or Tracey.

Snobs love to show off, and party planners, florists and couturiers have found that lavish spenders are on the increase. There are now said to be 100,000 millionaires in Britain. There are penthouse flats in London going for up-wards of £3m and the £1m house has even arrived in Bournemouth, which is the natural habitat of the snob. As a footballer's wife said to me, 'Round here they don't say "Come for drinks", they say "Come for cocktails".' There are more snobs, social climbers, rich northerners, bidets and Jacuzzis per acre in Bournemouth than anywhere else in the country. It's the land of gold medallions, Rolls-Royces and bronzed men with bouffant hair, who all look like Max Clifford and give poolside parties with lots of pretty girls in ankle chains and white bikinis.

Parties are beset with difficulties for the socially insecure. Johnny Roxburgh runs the Admirable Crichton, which organizes gloriously stylish parties, and he says, 'Customers want a display of lushness and abundance.' He planned Sting's wedding celebrations and recently staged a party with a dance floor constructed entirely of glass and another with a 40ft waterfall in the centre of the room. Then there was the 1950s theme party on a 390ft yacht where the dance floor was a revolving replica of a 78 record and everything down to the loo-roll holders was genuine Bakelite kitsch. There are party-givers to whom money is no object and Johnny orchestrated one which cost £900,000. He is a party planner and it's naff to call someone like Johnny's company 'the caterers'. I only did it once and he looked pained. He is brilliant and stately and frequently employs very posh people, including Princess Michael's son, Frederick. Johnny did the weddings of both my daughters and he and the waiters were far grander than the hostess.

Princess Michael is a snob on a major scale and even the Queen, who detests her, said, 'Oh, she's far too grand for us.' When the Princess goes to any public engagement, one of her staff lets the organizers know in advance what kind of flowers she wishes to see in the presentation bouquet. Evidently carnations, or anything orange, would offend her sensibilities.

Princess Michael more than anyone makes it obvious that accents are influential. She is the daughter of the late Baron Günther von Reibnitz and spent most of her childhood in Australia. When she came to Britain she changed her Aussie accent into husky foreign tones which helped her ensnare a prince.

Snobs are born, not made, and don't need any excuse to boost their determination to march up the social scale. A true snob never rests because there is always a higher goal to attain, a posher friend to emulate and more and more people to look down upon. I'm quite prepared to be scathing about three-piece suites, antiqued leather, chiming doorbells, patios, rubber plants and French marigolds, with the passionate contempt of a *nouveau*. Snobs are brilliant at enhancing everything in their lives with the breadth of vision of a successful estate agent. 'Lynda, do you mean balcony?' said the late Sir David English when I talked about my London terrace. 'Yes,' I said. I used to say I lived in Bushey, when in fact I lived in the socially inferior Bushey and Oxhey. However, this was no great leap of imagination for a social climber who, in a desperate attempt to keep her end up at a posh party, talked about 'my childhood on the estate', without making it clear that it was a council estate. Also, I know a very successful, highflying businesswoman who grew up in a council house in Dogsthorpe on the outskirts of Peterborough. When asked where she lived, she thought of Earl Spencer pronouncing Althorp 'Althrupp' and said Dowthrupp. Those who were born in the city itself are called Peterborians which always sounds very grand.

Snobs call a shed 'the garden room' because snobs, as somebody shrewdly said, want to level up not down. They buy leather-bound books by the yard and think they are madly egalitarian when they call the milkman Frank. If he, in turn, called them Michelle or Jennifer they would be none too pleased. They can quote fluently from book reviews rather than the books. They call the five rhododendron bushes at the bottom of the garden 'the wood', the au pair 'the nanny' and talk about the garden as 'the grounds'.

Snobs would sooner their daughter married a dissolute son of an earl than the capable child of a labourer. 'The plebs have all the money these days,' they drawl when their daily saves up for ten days in Benidorm.

They assume that anyone with a title is unparalleled for his wit, humour and personal charm. Princess Margaret only has to say 'Fancy' and everyone thinks she's a wit. On one occasion, she walked out of the wrong exit at a party and said, 'Wrong door,' whereupon everyone roared with sycophantic laughter and said, 'Oh, you're so amusing, Ma'am.' Snobs always put the word 'little' before any man or woman who they see as their social inferior. 'Such a nice little man,' they say patronizingly about their decorator, plumber or electrician. Occasionally, little people get sick of being looked down upon and turn nasty. This is what happened to children's novelist Noel Streatfeild after she sacked her little dressmaker. When the woman left, she turned to Noel's maid Rose and said, 'I'm afraid Miss Streatfeild will regret dismissing me as I'm a witch.' The following day the chandelier crashed from the drawing-room ceiling, two vases full of flowers fell from the table and a coffee pot toppled over and emptied itself onto Noel's bed.

'Have you told anyone you're a lord yet?' the late Lord Arran's wife always said whenever they went anywhere new. 'No,' he'd reply, 'but I'll get it in as soon as I can.' He was a realist and knew that his title invariably provided him with advantages, be it in service or attitude. He was used to getting his own way, and when a neighbouring girls' school erected a building which spoilt his view, he wrote to the headmistress and said that if she didn't pull it down instantly he'd go round and rape them all.

An ancestor of the Duke of Portland dismissed any servant who had the temerity to look at him. And people in Dorset still remember one rich old aristocrat who used to insist that council workmen cutting the hedgerows stand to attention and look at the ground when she was driven past by her chauffeur.

Joyce Grenfell, who was the niece of Lady Astor, was fairly snobbish when she was young. But as she grew older she became critical of some of her friends who came from identical backgrounds. One evening, when having dinner in a restaurant, she was revolted by their loud, unselfconscious, booming voices. 'They were really rather terrible,' she wrote later to a friend. 'I felt ashamed of my class and disassociated myself from it. It is the total disregard of other people that is so unattractive. And so arrogant. I do think it's time there was a social change. Roll on the tumbrils.'

Some exceptionally stupid snobs assume that all blue-collar workers and foreigners are inferiors. There was a famous occasion when a Pakistani gentleman walked into a Hampshire doctor's crowded waiting room and opened the door of the surgery. An irate woman grabbed him by the arm and said in condescending, pidgin English, 'You take turn. You in England now. Do as English do.' The man, who had been educated at Stowe, said in deliberate, equally pidgin English, 'No. You after me. Me doctor. Understand?'

Snobs look down on all reporters, seeing us as grub-digging inferiors. 'What right do these people have to have opinions?' demanded Princess Michael. A few years ago I was invited to be guest of honour and chief speaker at a lunch at the Majestic Hotel in Harrogate. When I arrived, I went into the Ladies to tart myself up and sat down on the only chair in front of the dressing table. 'Are you Press?' asked a lady with a rigid bust. 'Yes,' I said, mildly irritated by her superior tone, and unwisely added, 'And what are you?' 'I,' she said grandly, 'am a guest, and I do feel that as you're Press, you ought to leave the chair for the invited guests.' During lunch, I fixed her with what I thought was a gimlet eye and when I got up to speak hoped that she'd be utterly mortified. However, she was far too thick skinned. At the end, she came up to me, thumped me on the shoulder and thundered, 'I say, you are a card.'

When Fergie married Prince Andrew, all reporters with

passes into Westminster Abbey for the wedding were given a dress code by Buckingham Palace. The men had to wear morning suits and the females were instructed to wear formal frocks with hats and gloves. Clutching our notebooks, we then had to clamber up a flimsy ladder and sit on a rickety, temporary platform looking down on the proceedings. It was a bit like being told to dress up for the ball but being kept in the servants' hall. It was a total farce and in keeping with their marriage.

The worst kind of snobs are breakfast television presenters who grow too big for their boots. Television mogul Bruce Gyngell met a group of new presenters and prophesied, 'In six months, 90 per cent of you will have turned into monsters.' When talking about press photographers, one breakfast presenter instantly puts on a cockney accent, implying that every newspaper snapper is working class, ill educated and dim, which can't please Lord Lichfield. She also has an infuriatingly patronizing habit of saying 'Bless her' whenever anyone old, thick or lower class appears on the programme.

Most of us who want to be posh also want to be smart, unlike Margaret Beckett, the Leader of the House of Commons, who goes on caravanning holidays with her husband. 'We rather pride ourselves,' she says, 'on not being smart.' This is a bit like some rich people, who are so determined not to be seen as getting above themselves that they serve beer, prawn cocktails, steak and chips and Black Forest gâteau at their wedding receptions. They think they are being droll and amusing but all their poorer relatives are furious because they'd been expecting smoked salmon, oysters and champagne. Having bragged for weeks about their glamorous invite, they go back to work and are asked by their envious workmates for a blow-by-blow account of the occasion. They are too ashamed and embarrassed to say they'd had the kind of dinner you would get in a Southend pub.

I am not so much an *arriviste* as someone who is forever struggling upwards but never quite getting there. My daughters both have elegant houses and, occasionally, I find myself bearing a deeply shaming resemblance to Hyacinth Bucket. I'm afraid I have been on the verge of saying, 'I'm just off to visit my London daughter. The one with the terrace and the huge wrought-iron gates.' This isn't boastfulness but the fact that I'm quite impressed myself. I have a fairly smart garden, designed by a disciple of Gertrude Jekyll, but, on the day our tennis court was completed, I met someone who had their own cricket pitch.

I grew up in a house that had cast-off furniture inherited from my granddad. I actually thought that new furniture was a sign of being a bit of a toff, so you can see how much I've progressed. If you are born upper class, generally you stay there unless you are foolish enough to marry beneath you. I have absolutely no patience with heiresses who marry the chauffeur, or the shy plain daughters of tycoons who marry their hairdresser because he flatters them and pretends to listen. Margaret Austen, who was married to the Chief Executive of the London store Liberty, had an affair with her painter and decorator and lived to regret it. Always fornicate upwards, is my advice. I'm just as intolerant of the Marquess of Bath who had affairs with sixty-nine wifelets, mostly from lower-middle-class backgrounds.

Frank McCourt made a fortune from writing about his working-class Irish background in *Angela's Ashes*. However, he didn't do it until he was in his sixties. 'I didn't want to write about my miserable childhood,' he says, 'because we were ashamed of it. I couldn't have written about my mother while she was alive. She hated me uncovering the past. The only place for confession, she thought, is to a priest.' Instead, her shrewder son has become a millionaire by revealing the squalor and deprivation of his youth. He is not absolutely confident saying, 'You don't walk tall out of the slums.' But there is no doubt that when you are rich and famous there is a certain kudos and glamour in having come from the slums. If you stay there for the rest of your life then it remains soul-destroying and depressing. In one way or another, the effects of our childhood last for ever.

In my early married days, I went to a cocktail party and during a conversation with a woman festooned in diamonds, I said that I came from a working-class background. She stepped back in revulsion and couldn't have looked more horrified if I'd told her I had typhoid and had murdered my granny. 'Oh no,' she gasped, 'why do you say that?' I said, because it was the truth, but her horror was symptomatic of her own shame about her background. I discovered later that she'd worked in a fish and chip shop in Bolton and married a rich elderly bookmaker who had conveniently died and left her his fortune. She bought a vast bungalow in Bourne-mouth's Branksome Park, filled it with chandeliers, changed her name from Dot to Dorothea and reinvented herself. Only her housekeeper knew the truth because, every time her employer found a speck of dust, she lost her temper and screamed in her old, strident, northern tones. Inciting some-one to lose their temper is a very reliable way of finding out what their real accent is. It's very difficult to have a slanging match in a false accent. If ever I turn nasty, it's in a Lancashire voice. Even my phrases become northern and I'm not averse to shouting daft insults from my childhood along the lines of 'Got your eye full? Get your other eye full!' Personally, I yearn to be smart and possess natural authority. I'm so lacking in authority that, even after thirty years' service, when I forgot my pass to get into the *Daily Mail* offices, a security officer wouldn't let me in without signing the book. When I went to interview Barbara Cartland, I stopped a jogger to ask the way to her mansion. 'The main gates are at the end of the road,' he said. 'You'll want the tradesman's entrance.' I was driving an open-top BMW but clearly gave out powerful signals saying, 'This is a subservient person.' I felt as the mega-rich and brilliant Sue Townsend, creator of Adrian Mole, did when she went to book a room at London's Strand Palace Hotel. 'Are you aware of our minimum rates?' asked the receptionist. Sue blushed and her eyes filled with tears as she said, 'Oh dear, do I look as though I can't afford the minimum rates?' Actually, she could afford to buy the whole hotel but, as she says, 'You can't take the working-class girl out of you, can you?' I am sure she's right and, however much we prosper, there is a fundamental lack of confidence in most of us that never quite goes away.

Michael Caine is the son of a fish porter and a young reporter asked him, 'Were you very poor when you were young?' The famous actor said, 'Only in money, everything else we had. We had enough food, love and confidence.' During the war, he and his brother were evacuated from London to Norfolk. His mother then got a job as the cook in a Georgian manor house set in 200 acres. 'I had a sort of *Upstairs Downstairs* childhood,' he says. He was allowed to have leftovers from the kitchen, and developed a taste for pheasant, caviar and wine. His proud, strong father died from cancer of the liver and was so emaciated his son carried him into the ambulance as though he were a baby. When he died, he left thirty-six pence, after a lifetime of hard and brutal work. Michael Caine vowed to become so successful and rich that his family would never be poor again. Now he lives like a lord and has exquisite taste in art, fine wines and antique English furniture. He has an easy rapport with people from all backgrounds but insists that his employees call him Mr Caine. He's proof that it is foolish to judge the wealth of anyone by their accent. When he'd made his first million but wasn't yet an instantly recognizable face, he went into a Rolls-Royce showroom in Park Lane. 'How much is a Rolls-Royce?' he asked in his cockney accent. The commissionaire said sarcastically, 'How many do you want? Stop mucking me about. Clear off.' A livid Michael Caine then went to another dealer and bought a Rolls convertible. He got his chauffeur to drive him past the original showroom with the top down. The actor stood up and gave the commissionaire a two-fingered salute. His great friend Roger Moore teases him that the richer and more successful he becomes, the more cockney he gets. He owns several restaurants, is revered by his peers and is married to an exceptionally beautiful wife. He has a London flat with a spectacular view over the Thames, and a 200-year-old country house in Surrey. 'I'm every bourgeois nightmare,' he says. 'I'm a cockney with intelligence and a million dollars. They think they should have done it but then why didn't they if they were so much smarter and more intelligent than this stupid cockney git? So their revenge is to say, "He's not a real actor, he's a cockney actor." The attitude is "good ol' cockney go down the pub and have some jellied eels Michael." I haven't been in a pub since God knows when and I've never had jellied eels. I couldn't eat them, it would be horrible.' When he first went into the theatre, he was told that he would never get work as an actor until he learned to talk posh. He said, 'I'll show you how to be an actor without talking posh.' And with pride and bloody-mindedness he did exactly that. Michael Caine is mega-rich, mega-famous and probably the most bankable British actor in the world. He has style, confidence and panache but still, buried deep inside him is a certain irritation about the way he's perceived. When he was awarded an Honorary Fellowship of the British Academy of Film and Television Arts, he made a surprising speech which exposed an astonishing amount of anger and vulnerability beneath his urbane exterior. He revealed that he still feels an outsider and a loner. 'I became an actor in a youth club in South London,' he said. 'I never went to drama school because I came from a section of the community that never knew that there was such a thing. I had an awkward voice and a duff accent at a time when people were writing plays about chaps coming through french windows in cricket jumpers shouting, "Bunty's having a party."' Afterwards, the movie star was ridiculed for having a chip on his shoulder but he also said, 'I never really felt I belong in my own country and my own profession. All the way through, I have kind of felt on the outside as though I were just trying to make something of myself, and with very little help along the way. It has been cold out there.' Since he's now been knighted, possibly he finally feels he does belong. 'Sticks and stones can break my bones,' we used to chant in my youth, 'but words can never hurt me.' They can, of course, but we must press on and rise above it. This is an attitude close to Michael Caine's heart and he tells his two daughters, 'When something goes wrong don't accept it's a bloody disaster. Think positively and say, "Now what can I get out of this?" And you'll find there's always something.' It's wise advice. My three children are all writers, so whenever one of us, mostly me, makes a cracking fool of ourselves we say, 'That will be good for the novel.' Certainly I never waste an insult.

Violinist Nigel Kennedy had a different attitude and changed his middle-class voice into a South London accent. Cilla Black lost her Liverpudlian accent when she first arrived in London and then shrewdly reverted back to it when she became loved as 'Our Cilla'. However, her husband Bobby always insisted that she be addressed formally by their staff as Mrs Willis.

Sue Townsend is a working-class girl with top-class breeding who has not, unlike many pop stars, become arrogant with fame and wealth. 'I didn't even see garlic until I was thirty,' says Sue. 'I'm still frightened of it, and I wouldn't know where to begin with artichokes. Thank heaven they are out of fashion. Being mocked is my biggest fear though God knows I'm good material.' I'm in the same boat and once chomped my way through an entire artichoke without realizing you are meant to eat only the soft bits at the ends of the leaves.

Asparagus at grand dinner parties makes me very anxious and so do canapés. They are too big to eat at one go, but if I bite into them, they always fall to bits. I watch other people tucking into them with gusto and feel terribly envious. The dean at one of the Oxford colleges used to test interviewees by giving them a rimless bowl of cherries to eat to see what they did with the stones. If they spat them on to the floor they were offered a place. If they left them in the bowl they were on the possible list. If they put them in their pocket or swallowed them they were shown the door and marked down as humble people of low breeding who had no place in an élitist college.

Without a shadow of a doubt I'd have put them into my handbag and, indeed, probably still would. This does not fill me with shame. I'd do it because I wouldn't want to litter someone else's carpet with cherry stones. Unfortunately, this would provoke contempt not gratitude.

The truth is that you can do almost anything if you do it with panache and confidence. When I had lunch with Lady Vestey, she decided she wanted tomato sauce and the very stately butler carried in a bottle of ketchup on a large silver tray. My tomato sauce is homemade from fresh tomatoes, simmered with oregano and basil. But I'm only trying to prove I'm smart. Lady Vestey knows she's smart. I bet she could even make caravanning smart. Things are judged in social terms not by the deed but by the perpetrator. In recent years, Michael Caine has become a tremendously successful restaurateur. He knows how touchy people are about feeling that they are eating at the best table. So when a restaurant is newly opened, he eats at what is in truth the worst table in the room with his wife Shakira. Once it's established as Michael's table, all the guests are perfectly happy to use it. I took John Osborne to the Ivy and we were put next to the door leading to the kitchen. 'I see we're at the Tiger Bay end,' he said. Jeffrey Archer invariably gets a good table in most establishments because he's said to be the best tipper in London.

Aplomb is very much an upper-class characteristic as the Two Fat Ladies, the late Jennifer Patterson and Clarissa Dickson Wright, demonstrated. They both had the stentorian voices of upper-class gals and overwhelming charm. 'Look at those powerful shoulders,' Jennifer said admiringly to me as we watched Clarissa striding down the street. She's incredibly strong, with a formidable temper.

She knocked out a mad Alsatian with a right hook and put a mugger into intensive care. She also proves that when you are upper class neither alcoholism nor penury can give you an inferiority complex. She's coped with both with a kind of magnificent insouciance and a belief that something would always turn up.

I joined the ladies when they were filming one of their programmes in Llandudno and they nearly caused a riot on the pier. They were mobbed by working-class, old-age-pensioner groupies and Jennifer waltzed around the pier with a retired miner as the organist played 'The Blue Danube'. Then a besotted stallholder presented her with a box of whisky-flavoured fudge. 'I can't touch that,' boomed Clarissa, who has now been on the wagon for more than a decade. Her father was Sir Arthur Dickson Wright, who was the Queen Mother's doctor and a leading surgeon at London's St Mary's Hospital. When he interviewed medical students, he would have a rugby ball balanced on an open drawer in his desk. As the student stood up at the end of the interview he'd pick up the ball and throw it at them. If they dropped it they were turned down. If they caught it they were in with a chance. If they drop-kicked it into the wastepaper basket they were offered a place.

When Clarissa was introduced to the Earl of Selkirk, he'd never seen the *Two Fat Ladies* cookery programmes. 'What do you do?' he asked Clarissa. 'I'm a Fat Lady,' she said. 'Oh you shouldn't put yourself down like that,' said the kindly Earl. 'You might need to lose a little weight but I don't think it needs to be all that much.' It must have been the first time in her entire life that the magnificent Clarissa had ever been perceived as shy and insecure. In her youth, she plotted to kill her monstrous father. She used to drink two bottles of gin a day, and on one occasion had to be forcibly removed from the Ritz. She was carried out, sitting on her chair, by four police officers and taken to the nearest cells. Here she sobered up and spent the night giving legal advice to a young prostitute. Clarissa feels quite at home anywhere. She has never in her life felt humiliated, demeaned or a failure. An inability to be embarrassed by disaster, poverty or making a fool of oneself is a great upper-class strength.

When I travelled on the train with Clarissa and Jennifer, we went past endless rows of mobile homes on the coast near Rhyl. 'What on earth are those?' said Jennifer. 'They're sort of little houses where people come with their children and have holidays,' said Clarissa. 'What a perfectly ghastly idea,' said Jennifer. 'Why on earth do they want to do that?' 'I suppose they like it,' replied Clarissa. 'How extraordinary,' said Jennifer.

Snobs are to be found in all social classes as there is something very satisfactory about feeling superior and in the know. Most people wouldn't admit to it and say things like, 'It's just that we have high standards.' The upper class despise the middles for caring what people think, the middles look down on the lower middles for trying to be refined and the lower middles look down on the working classes for being rough. Meanwhile, the working class looks down on those who do not work, do not wish to work and think the state owes them a living, a car, a weekly crate of lager and an annual booze-up in Butlins.

ARE YOU A SNOB?

Yes No

1 Would you cringe if your son's fiancée said, 'Pleased to meet you'? ☐ ☐

2 Is the first thing you ask a new boyfriend, 'What does your father do?' ☐ ☐

3 Do you think you must be a lovely person because you're polite to waiters? ☐ ☐

4 Would you fancy a girlfriend more if her father were a duke? ☐ ☐

5 Would you be appalled if your daily called you by your Christian name? ☐ ☐

6 Do you check the label on somebody's coat when they hang it up? ☐ ☐

7 Did you join the Country Landowners Association as soon as you owned the minimum requirement of 10 acres (and display the accompanying sticker in your car window)? ☐ ☐

8 Do you ever sneer about a colleague by saying 'MPSIA', meaning, 'Minor public school, I'm afraid'? ☐ ☐

9 Would you mock someone for having a coach lamp outside their suburban front door? ☐ ☐

10 Would you be horrified if your daughter
    went out with the son of a labourer?   ☐ ☐

If you answered 'yes' to any of these questions
    you're a snob.

4

POPOCRACY AND ROYALTY

Many of the stars who make mega-money out of entertainment, be it in sport, movies or the rock and pop world, choose to live in the style of the landed gentry of an earlier age. They are the *nouveau* aristocracy or popocracy.

There are over 100,000 millionaires in Britain and their numbers have virtually doubled since 1992. They come from all social and educational backgrounds, from Eton and from comprehensives. Money frees us from the strictures of poverty but it doesn't necessarily change our tastes or habits. Lottery winners indulge their dreams and live in large ornate houses with orange carpets, wrought-iron dining tables, gilt cherubs and trailing plastic plants. Look at any social gathering and, invariably, people come from similar income groups. Doctors socialize with accountants and dentists. Milkmen drink with painters and decorators and dukes invite other aristocrats to their dinner parties. The reason working-class lottery winners are initially so unhappy is because they are catapulted overnight into a different social group. Their old friends are jealous and their new neighbours are often mocking and mistrustful. When working-class accounts clerk Jackie Green won £10m on the lottery she bought a £500,000 house in a posh area of Cheshire. She then married a Caribbean limbo dancer called Shannon. 'The neighbours never really took to Jackie,' said her mother, 'and they haven't taken to Shannon either.'

The recession is over and people are spending money as never before. Asprey and Garrard, the London jewellers, had no problem selling £50 sterling silver party poppers in the run up to the millennium. In the first month of the new century, dozens of yachts, priced well over £100,000, sold at the London Boat Show.

The behaviour of all of us is affected by the way we are treated. Rock and pop stars are worshipped, adored, fêted and indulged so they quickly ape the arrogance of old-fashioned aristocrats. Their wives are the ones sitting on the front row at all the couturier collections. They rarely have to pay for the clothes they order because designers are more than happy to lend a frock for a night in exchange for publicity. There is, after all, a fair chance it will get snapped by newspaper photographers and make the front pages. Rock stars like Mick Jagger are the ones with butlers, chauffeurs and head gardeners looking after the herbaceous borders. Several of them tried to appropriate the services of butler Paul Burrell after the death of Diana, Princess of Wales. They also employ Norland nannies for around £15,000 a year plus full board, their own room and the use of a car.

'You can tell a gentleman by his shoes,' said one-time hooker Monica Coghlan, who insists she was paid for sex by Jeffrey Archer. Maybe prostitutes have lower expectations about what constitutes a gentleman but speed and cash probably come high on their list of priorities. These days, the self-made rich are more likely to be wearing trainers than highly polished shoes so you can no longer tell a millionaire by either his shoes or the cut of his jib. Chris Evans always looks like the kind of down-and-out who in the old days might have been employed as a drive sweeper at grand houses. He grew up in Warrington and was only twelve when his father was diagnosed with colon cancer. The young Chris used to push him around the streets in a wheelchair but a year later his father died. Chris Evans has now spent £6m on Hascombe Court in Surrey, which was built for a descendant of the Duke of Atholl. It has 172 acres, four staff cottages, stables, a tennis court and swimming pool. Friends say he will probably just spend the occasional night there. He only has 172 acres, so he's not entitled to develop the squire's gait. This has been described by diarist James Lees-Milne as 'a walk of great confidence and quiet authority with a slight lilt of the bottom', but is only justifiably possessed by those who own 5,000 acres or more. Similarly, when an official at Ascot was asked how to spot a toff he said, 'Look for the aristocrat's gait, a sort of half-shuffle walk, as though they're carrying an invisible ceremonial sword.'

Mick Jagger is a popocrat. He grew up in a lower-middle-class house in Kent but owns the kind of property that only aristocrats owned in the past. He has a massive town house in New York and a French château, La Forchette, in the Loire Valley. His ex-wife Jerry Hall now lives in the exquisite Downe House in Richmond, which has glorious views over the Thames, with Windsor Castle on the horizon. He also has Stargroves, which is a £5m estate on Mustique in the West Indies. Ironically, he's selling it because the island has come down in the social world. Mick Jagger is said to detest the ostentatious vulgarity of the newly built house of his new neighbour, American fashion designer Tommy Hilfiger. And shock horror, a lot of houses on Mustique are owned by American, German and Japanese corporations or wealthy businessmen. Viscount Linley sold the house Princess Margaret gave him to avoid death duties and bought a château in Provence. David Bowie has also sold his house on the island. Meanwhile, Mick Jagger is thinking of buying an entire island off the South American coast. Unlike many rock stars, he's extremely careful with money, which is more a characteristic of the genuine aristocrat. One elderly peer, who bought all his bespoke shirts from Turnbull & Asser, used to take his fraying underpants in a carrier bag to have them darned. Now that the shop is owned by Mohammed Al Fayed, I am sure this facility is no longer available. I worked there for three days in order to write a piece about it for the *Daily Mail*, and the staff (though not all the customers) were gentlemen. One man was employed solely to iron the shirts and observing him was to watch an artist at work.

Like the old-fashioned aristocracy, pop stars want isolation and space. They then of course become removed from the pressures and reality of normal life. They begin to think they can behave in any way they wish because they are surrounded by lackeys who kowtow to their every whim. Paul Gascoigne is part of the same group and continually behaves with vile rudeness and indifference to anyone else's feelings. On the morning of his wedding, he appeared for breakfast in the hotel restaurant wearing only a towel around his waist. Later, he sat in the back of the car taking him to church, drinking champagne and making faces at passers-by.

Posh Spice and David Beckham have bought a mansion in Hertfordshire and have total confidence, brought by money, fame and acclaim. On one visit to Tesco to buy a pineapple, Posh was so appalled by the long checkout queue that she asked store officials if she could go straight to the front of the line. They agreed, and after queue-jumping she ran out to her chauffeur-driven car. Like many people who become mega-famous and immensely rich, she's grown increasingly alienated from ordinary human beings. The couple married at

Luttrellstown Castle outside Dublin and, during the reception, sat apart from the guests on thrones with baby Brooklyn. He was named after the American city in which he was conceived, which is pretty naff.

The popocracy has an incredibly low boredom threshold which is why they are always buying the latest craze, be it a watch, handbag or the latest F1 McLaren sports car for £600,000. They leave heaps of designer clothes and shoes worth thousands of pounds unworn and unopened in their bedrooms.

Spice Girl Mel B now owns the £3m seventeenth-century manor in Little Marlow, Buckinghamshire. The title of Lord and Lady of the Manor goes with the house, so one interesting question is 'If you are mistress of the manor are you necessarily a lady?' The answer is 'No', although Mel B did ring the Kennel Club to ask if a chocolate-coloured Labrador would be a suitable dog for a lady. And the answer to that is 'Yes' – if she's a country lover who likes hearty walks in all weathers. But if she's a girl from Leeds with a filthy temper, little patience, who loves the sun and is away from home for long periods, it's debatable. Mel B must be the first lady of the manor to pose in the nude for *The Sunday Times* when she was nearly nine months pregnant.

Elton John is the ultimate popocrat with his expensive clothes, ornate houses and royal guests. He, too, has entered the fantasy world where reality rarely encroaches. He has the courage to be vulgar and over-the-top without any inhibition, which might be why the royals are so fond of him. The Queen Mother was a guest in one of his houses which has views of Windsor Castle. She pointed to the flag which was flying from the castle and said, 'I see my daughter is at home.' In an interesting reversal of class roles Elton commissioned Viscount Linley to make him a £75,000 bed.

At his fiftieth birthday party, Elton wore a Louis XIV white and silver ensemble and an enormous curly wig which was so high he and his lover had to be transported to the party in a removal van. This was fitted with two thrones and decked out in velvet and gold. At one Elton bash, food was served on gold plates with gold forks and spoons which, I suppose, are the millionaire's version of gold taps. These are incredibly shaming and scream 'jumped-up' and 'nouveau'. His guests drank Laurent Perrier rosé champagne at £30 a bottle, which is preferable to rosé Asti spumante but still not a good idea if you want to be seen as a person of impeccable taste.

I've been snooty about pink champagne ever since I discovered it was the favourite drink of actress Julie Goodyear. She became famous as barmaid Bet Lynch in Coronation Street and embodies the worst characteristics of every class, which is quite an achievement. She has the vulgarity of the lower classes, the pretensions of the lower middle, the rudeness to her staff of the upper middles and the overwhelming arrogance of royalty. When I interviewed her at the Victoria and Albert Hotel in Manchester, there was a window which opened out over the canal. She was so irritating I had a passionate yearning to shove her out, which shows that my working-class belligerence isn't far below the surface. Indeed, my layer of urban sophistication is paper thin. After the interview, she gave me a wilting bunch of blooms which had seen better days. She left with her entourage and I got rid of a fraction of my rage by dumping the battered flowers in the wastepaper basket.

The only people who are not affected by the class system are those at the bottom of the social structure and those at the top. Those at the bottom can't go any lower and those at the top can't go any higher. 'We are forever being told we have a rigid class structure,' says Prince Edward. 'That's a load of codswallop. In many cases there are more opportunities than ever to do just about anything you want. The impression Britain gives is they can't wait to knock you down.' This was pretty rich coming from a man who got into Cambridge with such poor 'A' levels they'd have scarcely guaranteed a working-class boy a place at Loughborough. Like his Aunt Margaret, he wants to be royal when it suits him. He owes his education, income and most of his television productions to the fact that he is a prince. When his company strayed away from its royal subjects, they produced a flop in the abysmal series *Annie's Bar*.

Occasionally, Prince Edward goes to the United States to lecture and he attracts large audiences because his mother is Queen Elizabeth. He can afford his vast and ugly fifty-roomed Bagshot Park in Surrey because he's inherited wealth not because he's made it. Prince Edward more than anyone is powerful proof that the class system is alive and tremendously useful if you are born in the right cradle. It's also proof that we are still treated as who we are, not what we are. If Prince Edward weren't royal, he would probably be a bank clerk living in a semi-detached in Basingstoke and a passionate member of the local amateur dramatic society. Of course, in those circumstances he wouldn't be married to Sophie Wessex because he wouldn't be grand enough for this aspiring girl from Essex.

The royal family have the social confidence of those who are always treated with deference but they do behave in a way which in other people would be seen as really rather ghastly. They would be marked down as 'Horrors never to be asked again'. When they go to stay as guests, their hosts are told exactly what must be provided and what is required.

Princess Margaret sounds like the guest from hell. One hostess was asked to ensure that the bed in the Princess's room was pointing in a specific direction, which meant that all the furniture in the room had to be rearranged. She insists on strong lights, roaring log fires and somewhere to plug in her Carmen rollers. She likes pasta, chicken and lemon barley water.

Meanwhile, when the Prince of Wales goes to stay anywhere, the poor host receives a list through the post of the requirements of HRH. When it comes to food, the Prince likes soft-boiled eggs, wild mushrooms, pasta, fish, game, ice cream, soft cheese, French cheese, double cream, full-fat milk, Earl Grey, Laphroaig whisky and dry martini. This must be mixed with three parts gin to one part martini. He brings his own lavatory paper which is Kleenex Velvet. He likes to shower in the morning and bathe in the evening and wishes to be given a CV on every guest he is going to meet. He dislikes large portions, over-cooked vegetables, coffee, chocolate, nuts, garlic, curry, tropical fruit, oysters and blue cheese. I should think any hostess given these instructions feels an amalgam of irritation and anxiety. I wonder how the Prince would feel if his guests sent him a list of their needs in advance of their arrival and brought their own lavatory paper?

The royal family are always held up as an example of good breeding but they do many things which I would categorize as ill bred – always putting themselves first, for a start. Clearly, the royals are so accustomed to people being thrilled to meet them that it never strikes them that other people might be inconvenienced by their assumption that all that matters is their own welfare. Prince Charles, while anguishing about humanity as a whole, can be utterly self-obsessed and selfish when it comes to his staff. Richard Aylard, his former private secretary, was married with two children but even at home and off duty he was invariably on call and required to do his master's bidding. If he wishes to see anyone, the Prince often asks them to visit him for a brief chat at the inconveniently situated Highgrove. Alan Clark was just one extremely busy politician to be irritated by this royal imperiousness. The heir to the throne has a fortune of £290m so can easily afford the £150,000 a year he is said to lavish on his mistress, Camilla Parker Bowles. However, it is suspected that he gets her Versace frocks either on the house or cut price. His personal staff includes four valets, two chauffeurs, a baggage handler and two chefs.

HRH believes that, as Prince of Wales, he has to live up to a certain style and this is a style to which he has become accustomed. He has a love of extravagance – inherited from the Queen Mother – more suited to the nineteenth century than the twenty-first. Prince Charles lives like a king with shooting parties at Sandringham and deer stalking at Balmoral. He often borrows his grandmother's house Birkhall on the Balmoral estate, and when house guests arrive, they know they will step back in time at least half a century. They will be greeted as was Mrs Wallis Simpson when she went to stay at Fort Belvedere. There will be a retinue of servants in waiting with ladies' maids for the women and valets for the men. Bags will be unpacked, clothes pressed and baths drawn, with expensive bath oils, soap and shampoos provided. The wine will be of the finest and Prince Charles sometimes serves a first-growth Château Margaux at about £2,500 a case. The Prince's idea of recreation hasn't really changed since his grandfather's time. He loves hunting, fishing and polo. He takes friends on summer cruises although, unfortunately, on other people's boats. One great class divide is that if you can only afford a caravan in Clacton-on-Sea, you have to pay for it yourself. If you're filthy rich and royal then millionaires queue up to offer you luxurious freebies. Since there is no such thing as a free yacht, I think the only honourable response should be 'Thank you but I can't accept.' Unfortunately, there is a rather shamingly bourgeois, penny-pinching streak in the Windsors.

The Prince, of course, has been known to spend part of his summer holidays on the yacht of Greek billionaire John Latsis who lavishes millions on the entertainment of the rich and influential. The 455ft *Alexander* has countless staff and lush accommodation. On board there is a chandeliered ballroom, a night club, gym and billiard room. Three hundred tons of marble have been used for the Turkish baths but the yacht is owned by a vulgar man prone to offensive language, who boasts about his libido and has a fondness for lewd jokes. He was born into a poor family in the fishing village of Pyrgos. He's proof that if you can make enough money, no social barriers exist. He also seems to prove that our royal family can be bought. He provides the finest wines and rich food for his important guests and yet issued an edict saying that rations for his workers were to be limited. 'Nobody,' he said, 'can work well on a full stomach.' Clearly he thinks that the well-fed rich have no problem when it comes to playing and partying after a surfeit of expensive food.

Despite passionate criticism over the years, the royals, with a few minor changes, have carried on with their grand and indulgent lifestyle. The late MP Willie Hamilton made excoriating attacks on them to little avail. He called Princess Margaret 'an expensive kept woman who made a monstrous charge on the public purse with her languid life of favoured leisure'. His anger about privilege stemmed from his own poverty-stricken, working-class background in Durham as the son of a miner. 'I used to go to the local colliery and draw my father's pay,' he recalled. 'It was never more than a pound plus a few shillings and that was to keep six of us.' In 1941 when Hitler invaded Russia, he enlisted in the army as an ordinary soldier and then gained a commission rising to the rank of captain. He later felt ashamed of what he saw as class betrayal, although he conceded, 'It is easier to react about the injustices of privilege when others have it, but it is quite a different matter when you have it yourself.' All his life he remembered his early feelings of being intimidated by those of a different class. 'I had a hell of an inferiority complex,' he said. 'I felt we were inadequate somehow.' This kind of reaction makes strong people aggressive and weaker ones humble.

Willie Hamilton believed his own anti-royalist feelings stemmed from the 1926 strike. His father was out of work, he was at primary school and the children were all brought out on to the street to wave as a member of the royal family was being driven past in a grand limousine. 'I waved,' said Willie, 'but I resented the fine car because I knew we were so poor we hadn't enough coal for the fire.'

Willie Hamilton reserved much of his rage for the Queen Mother and it's not hard to see why. Despite her generous handout from the Civil List, in 1999 it was reported that she had an overdraft of more than £4m with Coutts, the royal bankers. Apart from the Queen, she is looked after by the largest personal staff within the royal family. She even has more than Prince Charles which takes some doing. House-keepers, butlers and gardeners are based permanently at her four residences, Clarence House, the Castle of Mey, Royal

Lodge in Windsor Great Park and Birkhall at Balmoral. The Queen Mother entertains with unrestrained extravagance and, like her grandson, is fairly liberal when it comes to her guests. Royals like to be entertained so are always drawn to amusing individuals even if they are not top toffs. The guest list is predominately male because, as one guest said, 'Frankly, Queen Elizabeth, just like her daughters, prefers the company of men.' She likes handsome chaps and is particularly fond of Charles Palmer Tomkinson, on whom Jilly Cooper is said to have based her irresistible character Rupert Campbell Black. HM invites between sixteen and twenty guests to lunch or dinner parties which she holds at least three times a week. Liveried footmen serve delicious food from huge silver platters, wine is poured into glittering crystal glasses and coffee served in priceless bone-china cups. Her cellar is said to contain vintage wine and champagne worth a queen's ransom. In May she holds fishing parties during her fortnight at Birkhall, and in July she has a house party at Sandringham. There are two house parties at her Scottish castle, Mey, in August and then it's back to Birkhall where she has house parties every week in September. Charades are played and there is much singing around the piano until the early hours of the morning. Stiff vodka martinis are served before lunch and the Queen Mother's intake is legendary 'She must have hollow legs,' said one staggered guest. The Queen Mother is always described as gracious and charming. If she had the same predilection for gin, frocks with feathers and lived in London's East End, she'd be a merry old soul who can certainly knock it back. Furthermore she would be known as a skinflint. She pays such meagre wages to her hard-worked staff that Prince Charles tops up the money of old retainers to the tune of £80,000 a year. The Queen also subsidizes her mother. 'It's not that the Queen Mother is mean,' says a courtier, 'it's just that she doesn't understand the costs of modern life.' If she'd had to manage like a working-class pensioner on a limited income, she would have been forced to understand or the heat and lighting would have been cut off and she would have had no money left at the end of the week for food.

If you are the Queen Mother, you can get away with being in debt and doing vulgar things without suffering from sneers. However, one peer of the realm did voice his opinion that 'It's extremely middle class of her to use fish knives.'

In addition to her four homes, the Queen Mother also has an apartment at Walmer Castle in Kent, which remains fully staffed although she only visits once a year. Whenever she travels, she is accompanied by a footman, two maids, two chauffeurs and a detective, provided by the Metropolitan Police. She serves vintage champagne at her regular extravagant dinner parties. She owns ten racehorses and, at Clarence House, she is looked after by vast numbers of staff. It is estimated she needs an income of £2 million a year to fund her grandiose lifestyle, which is surely excessive by anyone's standards. The royal residences are crammed with treasures but a confidante was reported as saying, 'You can't have the Queen Mother sending in a picture to Sotheby's every week.' I don't see why not. Other old ladies have to sell their engagement rings, their jewellery and, in a lot of cases, even their houses to pay for their nursing-home fees. When I wrote this in the *Daily Mail*, the majority of people agreed. However, there was a hard core, mostly old soldiers of all classes, who were incensed. They fought in the last war for King and country and the Queen Mother still epitomizes for them everything they risked their lives to protect. There was something very touching about old men ringing up a newspaper for the first time in their lives to try and articulate their deepest emotions. Most of them were living spartan lives on a pension. Their country had rewarded their patriotism with a cheap demob suit and £50. Despite this, they were passionate in their protective support for a rich, indulged, elderly woman. They continue to be grateful because she stayed in London with the King during the bombing and didn't go abroad to safety. Of course, ordinary citizens stayed because they had to, and neither expected nor got any praise for that. But the old men who, nearly sixty years ago, fought in mud and cold and saw their comrades die in front of them remained indomitable. They were and always will be fierce defenders of the Queen Mother. They are a dying breed with their patriotism, selflessness and respect for their leaders and, despite everything, I feel sad about that. On the telephone, they were polite and dignified. Most of them had been sergeants and corporals. It was the officers with posh, arrogant voices who were abusive. So what does this prove? Mostly that it takes more than a posh voice to make a gentleman.

5

NAFF AND NON-NAFF

Naff and non-naff is probably the millennium equivalent of Nancy Mitford's U and non-U. When she wrote her famous book *Noblesse Oblige*, it was virtually a handbook for those who wanted to ape the mores of the upper classes. People began saying 'sofa' instead of 'settee', 'looking glass' for 'mirror', 'writing paper' for 'notepaper', 'napkin' for 'serviette' and 'loo' for 'toilet'.

Are you naff and, if you are, do you care? Television presenter Wendy Turner and her husband, actor Gary Webster, obviously don't. They sold the photo rights of their wedding to *OK!* magazine. In order to protect their investment, the wedding invitations said, 'Due to the fact that Gary and Wendy have unashamedly sold their souls and the photo rights to their wedding to *OK!* magazine, guests are respectfully requested to leave the camera work to the official snappers or Gary and Wendy may not get their dosh, and we all want champagne not Asti, don't we?' Surely the only appropriate response for guests would have been to demand an attendance fee as they were likely to be used as extras in the pictures? The bride, of course, was pregnant, making one think the offspring ought to be called Justin for 'Just in time'. However, I suppose the days when brides who were married in white were presumed to be virgins are long gone. I thought it was a bit naff to have the wedding service at the Ritz and then bus the guests to a cheaper hotel for the reception. The bride wore a strapless dress which was cut so low at the back that she nearly had a cleavage behind. Her bridegroom wore a black shirt with a long velvet jacket and the pair bore an undeniable resemblance to the sheriff and a good-time girl in a Western movie.

Food and wine are the perfect areas in which to expose naffness. Cliff Richard has his own six-acre vineyard at his house in the Algarve. Since his idea of a treat is Smash potato with a tin of chilli con carne, I can only think his wine will be a Portuguese version of Liebfraumilch. His fans, of course, epitomize naffness. They have an affection for nylon overalls, Crimplene and backless mules. At home, they wear candle-wick dressing gowns and protect the three-piece moquette suite in the front room, which they call the lounge, with plastic covers. These match the plastic flowers which they keep on the sideboard next to the fruit bowl. They collect Spanish dolls and their gardens are full of gnomes with fishing rods and white polyester swans called Cliff. They have crazy-paving paths up to their front doors which are glass with wrought-iron motifs. They write love letters to their hero on lavender-scented, purple notepaper and keep his signed picture in a gilt frame on top of the television set. They love Bacardi and Coke or pina coladas and are enthusiastic ballroom dancers. They are particularly good at the rumba and their spiritual home is Tenerife. They are usually married to husbands who carefully lacquer their hair over their balding patch and are more often than not called Reg or Garry.

Naffness is to be found in all classes and incomes. It is not the prerogative of the lower classes as Princes Edward and Andrew frequently demonstrate. 'If you have a royal or aristo-cratic title it is assumed you don't have any brains,' Prince

Edward said petulantly. His wedding was a combination of ostentation and naffness. He dithered endlessly beforehand about whether or not he could make money out of his nuptials by getting his own company, Ardent Productions, to film the wedding and sell the video. The couple gave a pre-wedding television interview in the garden of their vast and ugly mansion. Unfortunately, they chose to do it sitting at a round table inadequately covered with a flowered tablecloth. Close up, this made them look as though they were sitting in the front room of a Skegness boarding house. When Sophie was asked about Diana, Princess of Wales, she said she sometimes looks at pictures and doesn't know whether it's her or Diana. The rest of us don't have that problem.

Sophie Wessex could be an Identikit for a games mistress in a minor girls' boarding school. She is authoritative and capable with inner steel, which appeals to the royal family who can't bear bleeding hearts. Her maiden name was Sophie Rhys hyphen Jones which, according to Victoria Mather, the Social Editor of *Tatler*, is terribly naff. 'It's like an elephant trap,' she says 'to catch the socially inept.' Evidently, it is much smarter to have a double-barrelled name without a hyphen as in Camilla Parker Bowles. In fact, the only reason my name has a hyphen is because it was inserted by accident on my husband's birth certificate. The rest of his family don't have one but my parents were madly impressed when I married a chap with a hyphen which just goes to show how wrong you can be.

After Emma Noble married James Major, she decided to call herself Emma Noble-Major which caused lots of upper-class sniggering. But then, John Major is used to mockery. After his autobiography was published, Nigel Lawson reviewed the book and described it as 'surprisingly well written'. He meant, 'I'm amazed that anyone who left school at seventeen and is the son of a man who made garden gnomes managed to write, let alone finish, a book.' Lord Lawson was educated at Westminster and Christ Church, Oxford and yet produced a tedious autobiography.

'Why do my sister's children keep marrying all these people who are so common?' asked Princess Margaret when Prince Edward married Sophie. Unfortunately, calling other people 'common' reveals an inherent vulgarity of one's own. Before the wedding, the 600 guests were given instructions about behaviour and dress, including the fact that they must not wear hats. It was a bit like the kind of bossy list you get before you go to boarding school for the first time. At the wedding breakfast, the royals got served but the other guests had to help themselves from a buffet. If you'd wanted to pick up any pointers on 'how to be posh', you would have found none at this wedding. The Queen was done up to the nines in mauve lace with feathers in her tightly permed hair and, with her rather porky middle, bore an unmistakable resemblance to Mrs Bott in the 'Just William' books. Mrs Bott is very rich, very vulgar, loves ostentation and is married to Mr Bott, who made his money out of inventing the nation's favourite sauce. A fondness for sauce is very naff unless it's in a Bloody Mary.

I went to interview Princess Anne at Gatcombe Park and saw that she displays every memento she has ever been given and they include some pretty ghastly things. I wouldn't give house room to African carvings or national dolls. However, if you're a royal and the daughter of one of the richest women in the country, you can get away with bad taste and terrible ornaments, particularly if everyone knows you have a mansion stuffed with inherited antiques.

I went to one naff supper party where the host went round filling glasses from a wine box. This wasn't surprising as it was to accompany lasagne cooked in a roasting tin. The late Pat Phoenix, who played Elsie Tanner in *Coronation Street*, also produced wine boxes at her very rare dinner parties. This was because, although she always looked as though she would be happy propping up the bar, she wasn't interested in alcohol of any kind. Wine boxes are naff even on a picnic and picnics are just as revealing as dinner parties. Paper plates and napkins are naff. So are egg or sardine sandwiches, sausage rolls, hard-boiled eggs or anything in Tupperware containers, which scream lower middle class. Posh people pack picnic baskets with game pies, home-grown asparagus and wild strawberries.

If you want to avoid the worst kind of vulgar decorative mistakes you could get a lot of tips about what not to do from the houses of newly successful footballers. They love sun lounges and white leather suites. They adore flock wallpaper, oak furniture, draped orange curtains, chandeliers, circular baths, water beds, cocktail cabinets which play *Nessun Dorma* and carpets with such thick pile you can't see your feet. You may think this sounds awfully snobbish but I'm trying to be factual. If you truly love and yearn to have a white leather sofa, then I'd be the first to say, 'Go out and buy it.'

Rich footballers and their wives have fancy kitchens with over-decorated pine and games rooms with a corner bar called Ye Olde Taverne where they serve rum and black. Their gardens have ornate rockeries, masses of pampas grass and a massive barbecue area on what they call the patio. Gardens reveal a lot about class and you would be unlikely to find an *Acer elegantulum* in a footballer's garden. This is the species of tree which Michael Heseltine has planted at his vast estate in Northamptonshire which is cared for by eight gardeners. He may have been mocked as a *nouveau* who had to buy his own furniture, but he's created his own arboretum, which is the kind of thing that nobs do. Mrs Heseltine is elegant, blond and understated, but footballers' wives wear strappy shoes with teeteringly high heels and trousers which are so tight you can see they're not wearing knickers. Most of them look as though they were hostesses at Stringfellows and, indeed, many of them were. Marrying a footballer or becoming a beauty queen is the way stunning working-class girls move away from council estates. The most successful and richest footballers have the most glamorous and toughest wives. Anybody who sneers at my theory that every single world has its own class system need only look at star footballers. The social status of the women is totally dependent on the value and professional talent of their chaps. The husbands, on the whole, hold the purse strings, which could be why they are more extravagant than their wives. When I interviewed Vinnie Jones, we spent the entire time talking about his purple suit and matching handmade shoes for his forthcoming wedding. This interest in fashion is absolutely alien to most aristocrats who are happiest in darned pullovers, battered Barbours and moth-eaten caps. In fact, Alec Douglas-Home, who was Tory Prime Minister 1963–4, was frequently taken for a gardener.

My own house in Dorset belonged to an old friend of the Queen Mother who previously lived in a Scottish castle. When her husband died, she wanted somewhere smaller which didn't need so many staff. So she bought the eight-bedroomed house with stables and a cottage and had a bungalow built for her chauffeur and his wife, who helped out with the cleaning. The gardener lived in the stables, the housekeeper in the house and, with the occasional addition of temporary staff, she managed to tough it out in her greatly reduced circumstances. An influential, alcoholic member of the Queen Mother's staff frequently came to stay and bribed the chauffeur to go out and buy him bottles of brandy. When the chauffeur drove his employer back to Scotland for visits, she would ask him to stop every three hours and say to him, 'Would you like to make yourself comfortable?' and he was expected to go behind a bush. This expression from a very posh lady sounds as vulgar as the dreadful phrase 'comfort stop', used by couriers on long coach trips. 'When in doubt, be blunt,' would be my advice. Anything arch or in doublespeak is naff. The same applies to good manners.

Naffness is pretension, bad taste and over-the-top ornateness. It's apparent in objects which are made to impress and not because they are of intrinsic good design. The best advice I was ever given was that things should be either beautiful or useful. Naff people have a predilection for collecting those awful Capodimonte figures or Swarowski crystal swans overdecorated with touches of gold. 'If wanting the best of everything means you're a snob,' the writer Elizabeth Jane Howard said to me, 'then I'm a snob.' When she and Kingsley Amis got married, she persuaded him to have his shirts custom made, but she couldn't persuade him to stop preferring the kind of dinners he'd been used to in his lower-middle-class childhood. She placed glorious food in front of him but he covered it in HP sauce. He also irritated her by belching loudly and carried on doing it just to convince her and possibly himself that she didn't intimidate him.

Unfortunately, if you are very clever and a highly esteemed novelist, you can behave with vulgarity, crassness or rudeness and people think you are droll and original.

Kingsley Amis left a party thrown by the late Lady Pamela Berry saying, 'Sorry Pam, got to go and have an injection in my arse.' Somerset Maugham would have approved as his advice to would-be writers was always 'Never use a long word when a short one will do.' Any kind of pretentious, convoluted speech is naff and so is boasting. Princess Margaret's son, David Linley, is the same age as Richard, the son of Laurence Olivier and Joan Plowright. When the boys were babies, Lady Olivier told the Princess that Richard had said his first word which was 'dada'. The Princess said, 'David's first word was "chandelier".' This was not one-upmanship as it would never occur to the Princess to think that she needed to compete. Obviously, she feels superior to us all, which is why she only ever does what she wants. If she is bored, she leaves a party, and in the old days, if she was having a good time she would dance all night and no one was expected to leave before she did. It never crossed her mind that others might have to work the following day. This insensitivity to other people is exceptionally vulgar, but it's a royal characteristic.

'What's wrong with being naff?' say some people who think the whole subject is ridiculous. The answer is absolutely nothing, as long as you're happy and your friends and family are not ashamed of you. Above all, only marry or cohabit if you find someone who feels the same or if one of you is prepared to let the other have all their own way. If you have opposing tastes, then someone has to be designated style guru or blood will be spilt. Actually, 'cohabit' is a pretty naff word. It's the jargon of social workers who rarely use plain, simple, straightforward English. In Noël Coward's novel, *Pomp and Circumstance*, the heroine talks about her seven-year-old son kicking his school friend between the legs with the result that his testicles are badly swollen. 'I just can't abide the word testicles,' says her irate husband. 'It's smug and refined like "commence" and "serviette" and "haemorrhoids". When in doubt always turn to the good old honest Anglo Saxon words. If you have piles say so. I should expect Nanny to say testicles.'

Nannies as a species yearn to be refined. They want their young chaps to be little gentlemen and the girls to be ladies. They teach them terrible lower-middle-class words and are so fussy about cleanliness and washing their hands that they give them phobias about germs. Nannies crook their little finger above their glass when they drink sherry and hand round what they call 'nibbles' if they have a party. They call two-year-olds 'toddlers', and say arch things like 'Back in the knife box Miss Sharp' if the five-year-old is cheeky.

When couples go to see the vicar before their wedding, he invariably talks about fidelity, loyalty, sex and children. He asks them endless questions but rarely the vital one: 'Have you got similar tastes when it comes to houses, furniture and décor?' There is little doubt that if one of you likes naff things and the other doesn't, divorce is on the cards. Money, sex and politics have never been any problem in my marriage but we've nearly killed each other over choosing a picture. Luckily, my husband comes from a family where the furniture and silver is inherited. The downside is that we have got some huge, unwieldy mahogany wardrobes which I would willingly chop up for firewood. I still resent the fact that my mother-in-law never even consulted me when she handed them over. When it comes to paintings, my solution now is to go off and buy the one I like so that it's a *fait accompli*. We can then have the row when it arrives rather than in public in the art gallery. Compromise is said to be the secret of happy marriages but it's the kiss of death when it comes to design. 'I like very simple lines and my wife likes fancy things and frills,' said one schoolteacher husband. 'We both give way a bit when it comes to buying furniture with the result that we never have anything either of us really loves.' Certainly their Yorkshire sitting room has the soulless feel of a Marriott hotel. The décor of this hotel chain is so dull that Michael Douglas didn't want to stay in the one in Swansea, even with Catherine Zeta Jones. Finally he conceded, but only after he'd paid for the entire suite to be 'refurbished'.

Marrying somebody from a different social background means that not only the wedding but the marriage itself will be a minefield. There is absolutely no common ground when the bride's father is to the left of Arthur Scargill and the bridegroom's mother is to the right of Genghis Khan. The arch snob Evelyn Waugh, who married upwards, said, 'I was early drawn to panache.' In these circumstances it's quite easy because someone like Waugh was more than anxious to take on the customs, friends and income of his wife's relations and class. It's when a working-class husband gets belligerent about his middle-class wife's family that the problems start. He's so determined not to lose face that he carries on drinking lager out of a can. Everyone else is sipping wine out of glasses, but he feels he has to make a point. Before the wedding, when the bride's mother insists on morning suits, he says, 'I'm not prancing around like some nancy boy.' In the end he gives in but gets his own back by calling his mother-in-law 'Ma'. The middle classes think this is incredibly common, but the upper classes often address their parents as Ma and Pa. Women find it much easier to adjust to a posher lifestyle than men because they don't keep feeling affronted. They are quite happy to be chameleons and blend in with their surroundings. Men feel slighted if they are criticized because they like to be in charge.

Leaving one's own class behind is always tricky and affects people in different ways. 'Of course the marriage was going to fail,' said Dame Barbara Cartland after the divorce of Earl Spencer and his wife, Victoria Lockwood. 'She doesn't come from the kind of background he's used to.' As Charles Spencer's background was wretched and dysfunctional, this seemed a damned good thing.

When John Major got married, he wore a morning suit. He told me it was because his mother-in-law insisted but he was always more upwardly mobile than his brother Terry, who married a wife called Shirley. Terry and Shirley, like Lynda, are very naff, lower-middle-class names. I'm sure I would be much more confident if I were called Francesca. I wonder if it's too late to change? Terry Major is partial to DIY and during John's premiership he became quite famous himself. He was an habitué of the party scene and a newspaper columnist and wrote a book about his family. He became a figure of fun and much ridiculed but he had his own dignity and never seemed to care. He rose above it, which is all that matters.

Dudley Moore went to Oxford as an organ scholar and he felt utterly traumatized. 'I come from a working-class home in Dagenham,' he says, 'and when I first arrived at Oxford I really couldn't open my mouth because everyone seemed frightfully suave and in control.' Eventually, he changed his voice completely, which no doubt irritated his mother who was a powerful character. Unlike the relatives of many celebrities, she never became in awe of her famous film-star son. She remained in her small house in Dagenham and gave no indication that she was impressed by Dudley's talent, wealth or success. He was at Oxford with the equally working-class Alan Bennett, who has used his northern diffidence, inhibition and self-consciousness to powerful effect in his writing. He is revered and critically acclaimed but retains his northern vowels and travels everywhere by bicycle. Posh voices still command respect and you get quicker service in bars and better treatment in shops.

If you are powerful, famous or rich then a regional accent can be part of your charm as illustrated by Michael Caine, Barbara Windsor and the late Labour Prime Minister Harold Wilson. However, if you are going to change it successfully, it's no use only half doing it because then you sound uncertain, unsure and as though you are trying too hard.

Accents do not hold anyone back once they are rich or successful but they can pigeonhole those at the bottom of the social scale. John Major wouldn't have been quite so mocked if he'd sounded like Douglas Hurd. On the other hand, he was chosen as leader in preference to the upper-class Mr Hurd. Nevertheless, we can't keep snobbishness down and there was much derision when it was revealed that the Majors used a Teasmade. 'I didn't know it was naff to have a Teasmade,' said Mrs Major. A decade after her husband became Prime Minister, she probably now knows that so are hostess trolleys and the peacock wicker chair in which she was so often pictured.

When Mr Major first became Prime Minister, his image was of Honest John, man of the people, although it was never as simple as that. He made it clear that he was not going to be packaged, prettified or improved. Unlike Harold Wilson and Maggie Thatcher, who both had expensive cosmetic dental work, he was not going to have his teeth capped. He was not going to have his wardrobe revamped or his personality jazzed up and he insisted on giving election speeches in the open air standing on a little box. Unfortunately, this made him look like a Boy Scout leader. His first publicized meal as Prime Minister was a fry-up at a service station on the M6. He refused to have any voice trainer brought in to untangle his strangulated South London vowels. He had at some time tried to change his accent but presumably he hasn't got a very good ear because he got it wrong. Despite his high office and formidable achievements, he had a kind of truculent chippiness which never left him. He carried on saying 'want' to rhyme with 'punt', though later on he began to rhyme it with 'pant'. It meant his speeches had less impact and the falseness of his vowels intruded on what he was trying to say. However, as someone who used to pronounce 'but' to rhyme with 'foot' and then with 'pat' and still has to pause before she gets it right . . . I'm in no position to mock.

Baroness Dean of Thornton-le-Fylde had a similar vowel problem but this has not held her back and the ex-Lancashire secretary, daughter of a railwayman, is one of Tony Blair's favourite peers. She lives in a £1m house in Islington with a £350,000 house on the waterfront at Falmouth. She and her husband are members of the Royal Cornwall Yacht Club and sail a 38ft £100,000 yacht. She was the first woman union head and in the early eighties was general secretary of SOGAT. Her tenacity, shrewdness and dazzling blonde looks took her to the top. When she was chairing important meetings, she utilized her shorthand speed of 160 words per minute and took her own notes. She's achieved power and status but never conquered her vowels. Vocally, she is stuck in a kind of naff no woman's land between Hyacinth Bucket and Margot in *The Good Life*. She would have been wiser to stick to her pure northern tones, as half-measures really are not a good idea.

Beryl Bainbridge says she would like to see all regional accents abolished because, in her opinion, they can be a handicap and impede success. I think life would be much less fun. Any upwardly mobile upstarts can always change their voices and leave the old accents behind.

TEN NAFF FOODS

1 Egg and chips
2 Prawn cocktail
3 Pineapple chunks
4 Anything flambéed
5 Hard-boiled eggs in salad
6 Tinned salmon
7 Scampi in a basket
8 Coleslaw
9 Pickled gherkins
10 Black Forest gâteau

SMART FOOD

1 Grouse
2 Homemade bread
3 Scottish lobster
4 Parma ham
5 Wild strawberries
6 Asparagus
7 Langoustines
8 Vichyssoise
9 Wild salmon
10 Clotted cream

SMART DRINKS

1 Vintage champagne
2 Lapsang Souchong
3 Real ginger beer
4 Gin and dry vermouth
5 Homemade lemonade
6 Sparkling elderflower
7 Freshly squeezed orange juice
8 Mint tea
9 Caffè latte
10 Hot chocolate

NAFF DRINKS

1 Asti spumante
2 Snowball
3 Snakebite (lager and cider)
4 Rum and blackcurrant
5 Malibu and pineapple
6 Mateus rosé
7 Liebfraumilch
8 Pernod and lemonade
9 Gin and orange
10 Ovaltine

NAFF REMARKS

1 Enjoy!
2 Pleased to meet you.
3 Chin chin.
4 Are there any more at home like you?

5 Charmed, I'm sure.
6 Meet my better half.
7 My compliments to the chef.
8 We've met before. I've seen you in my dreams.
9 You'll have to take us as you find us.
10 Cheers.

PUT-DOWN REMARKS

1 How big is your shoot?
2 I was amazed you weren't in the royal enclosure.
3 Have a peach. The gardener grew them in the peach house.
4 I'm going for my final fitting with Christian Lacroix.
5 We're getting married in our estate church.
6 We've lived here since the seventeenth century.
7 Glyndebourne's become so vulgar these days. Personally I much prefer Garsington.
8 Did you see Mummy's picture in *Tatler*?
9 I'm afraid he's MPSIA [Minor public school, I'm afraid].
10 My dear, he's so *nouveau* he's joined a shooting syndicate.

NAFF BEHAVIOUR

1 Putting Mrs, Ms or Mr in brackets when you sign your correspondence.
2 Leaving the television on when people arrive.
3 Buying your child a pair of Gucci bootees at £95 a pair.
4 Keeping napkins in napkin rings for the following day.
5 Sending out invitations to a child's party saying 'Carriages at 4'.

6 Loading the dishwasher before serving the pudding.
7 Saying, 'Take a pew.'
8 Talking about spending quality time with your children.
9 Using your mobile in a restaurant.
10 Getting your secretary to pp your letters.

NAFF ITEMS OF CLOTHING

1 Socks with open-toed sandals
2 Men's short-sleeved shirts
3 Anything in polyester
4 Ties with matching handkerchiefs
5 Double-breasted waistcoats
6 American tan tights
7 Ankle bracelets
8 Purple underpants
9 Cravats
10 Shell suits

NAFF NAMES

1 Sharon
2 Lynda
3 Tracey
4 Rita
5 Wayne
6 Hilda
7 Shirley
8 Kevin
9 Darren
10 Beryl

SMART NAMES

1 Ned
2 Kit
3 Theo
4 Anastasia
5 Arabella
6 Lucinda
7 Peregrine
8 Freddie
9 Edmund
10 Cosmo

NAFF WORDS

1 Bubbly
2 Snifter
3 Toilet
4 Dessert
5 Function
6 Pardon
7 Cruet
8 Lounge
9 Vestibule
10 Little girls' room

NAFF THINGS IN HOUSES

1 Tooled Moroccan leather pouffe
2 Teasmade
3 Hostess trolley
4 Coloured lavatory paper

5 Budgerigar in a cage
6 Net curtains
7 Chiming doorbell
8 Plastic lavatory seat
9 Cocktail cabinet
10 An MFI kitchen

SMART THINGS IN HOUSES

1 Library
2 Solid oak floors
3 A butler
4 Adam fireplace
5 Steel kitchen table
6 Le Corbusier chair
7 Antique grandfather clock
8 Ancestral portraits
9 Two staircases
10 Servants' hall

SMART THINGS IN GARDENS

1 Arboretum
2 Box hedges
3 Maze
4 Pleached lime walkway
5 Walled vegetable garden
6 Clematis
7 An old retainer
8 York stone paths
9 Wooden wheelbarrow
10 Laburnum tunnel

NAFF THINGS IN GARDENS

1 Patio
2 Busy lizzies
3 Gas barbecue
4 Mock-Victorian conservatory
5 Plastic Grecian urns
6 Pampas grass
7 Goldfish pond
8 Hanging baskets
9 Plastic garden furniture
10 Coloured concrete paving stones

SMART FIRST DATES

1 Summer lunch on the terrace at the Ritz
2 Fish and chips on the beach at Whitby
3 Dom Perignon on the grass at Lord's before watching the cricket from the Members' Pavilion
4 A walk ending with a flask of mulled wine on the white sands of the Isle of Bute
5 A summer picnic on the grass at Lulworth Castle before watching open-air opera
6 Breakfast at the Dulwich Picture Gallery
7 Lunch on Eurostar (first class) *en route* for Paris
8 Piloting own helicopter and landing at Gidleigh Park, Devon, for dinner
9 A walk along Dorset cliffs and evening picnic overlooking Worbarrow Bay
10 Anywhere with someone you fancy

NAFF FIRST DATES

1 A medieval banquet
2 A visit to a theme pub
3 Supper at a Harvester
4 A carvery anywhere
5 Arriving with a single red rose in cellophane and tickets
   for *The Mousetrap*
6 A trip in an air balloon
7 An invitation to watch a video with a takeaway vindaloo
8 A karaoke night
9 Tickets for the Millennium Dome
10 Anywhere with someone you don't fancy

SMART PETS

1 Chocolate-coloured Labrador
2 Llama
3 Abyssinian cat
4 Blue and gold macaw
5 Horse
6 Irish wolfhound
7 Falcon
8 Goat
9 Shetland pony
10 Humboldt penguin

NAFF PETS

1 Rottweiler
2 Goldfish
3 Tabby cat

4 Hamster
5 White mice
6 Tropical fish
7 Dachshund
8 Pot-bellied pig
9 Chihuahua
10 Ferret

SMART HOLIDAYS

1 Cape Cod
2 The Scottish Highlands
3 Provence
4 Winspit, Dorset
5 Deauville, France
6 Rock, Cornwall
7 'Cul na Shee' bungalow on the beach by Sadell Castle on the Mull of Kintyre
8 Frinton
9 Costa Smeralda, Sardinia
10 St Barts, Nevis

NAFF HOLIDAYS

1 Southend
2 Costa Brava
3 Great Yarmouth caravan park
4 Butlins
5 Package holiday to Lanzarote
6 Boarding house, Clacton-on-Sea
7 Tenerife
8 Disneyland, Florida

9 Blackpool
10 Magaluf

SMART HOBBIES

1 Croquet
2 Bridge
3 Polo
4 Fly fishing
5 Grouse shooting
6 Real tennis
7 Cricket
8 Opera
9 Tapestry
10 Chess

NAFF HOBBIES

1 Bowls
2 Pool
3 Bingo
4 Coarse fishing
5 Train spotting
6 Line dancing
7 Crazy golf
8 Football
9 Netball
10 Computer games

CLASSLESS HOBBIES

1 Painting
2 Golf
3 Walking
4 Piano playing
5 Squash
6 Snooker
7 Tennis
8 Gardening
9 Astronomy
10 Swimming

<u>6</u>
TACKY TOFFS AND MONSTERS

I was once involved in a television programme about class and the researcher asked me if I had a chip on my shoulder about being working class. I was amazed by the question and said with total confidence, 'No, absolutely not.' I'm proud of my family, my roots and my background. It gave me everything I possess in terms of common sense, pride, application and a belief that work is so much more fun than fun. I found the suggestion that I could have any chip absurd and a bit insulting.

Soon afterwards, I interviewed the exceedingly posh Tara Palmer Tomkinson and revised my opinion. She's the daughter of Charles and Patti Palmer Tomkinson who are close friends of Prince Charles. When Tara first came to London, her father bought her and her sister a London flat and gave them an allowance. Since then she's turned freeloading into a fine art and, because of her name, designers flock to give her their garments for free. She flies around the world to fashion shows and parties and rarely pays her own fare. If she ever did buy an economy ticket, she would, I'm sure, be instantly upgraded to club or even first class. She's testimony to the fact that the 'haves' get even more heaped upon them. After she appeared on Frank Skinner's show, the comedian, who comes from a working-class background, said, 'I could have summoned up a hundred years of class hatred and really torn into her.'

Tara is spoilt, very beautiful, indulged and completely out of touch with real life. She has two maids, including one who packs and unpacks for her. 'I know I could do it for myself,' she says, 'but the trouble is, I do it so badly. I'm always coming back from somewhere, different countries and things, so there are lots of bags. I need someone to sort them all out.' I found her upper-class self-assurance intensely irritating.

She said that she loathed snobs and was friendly to everyone. I resented her assumption that being civil to working-class people was a sign that she wasn't a snob. Her attitude was objectionable and patronizing. She said that one of the bouncers at London's Browns night club told her, 'You're the only one who's nice to us. You don't understand the shit we get from people.' Meanwhile, when the head waiter at Browns mentioned to her that he had always dreamed of going to Wimbledon, she said, 'Every year my father gets good seats on the centre court. So I'm going to make your dream come true, you're coming with me to Wimbledon.' She thinks this demonstrates that she's not a snob. She says:

> If I were a snob, I would never do that. A snob is a person who thinks they are better than those beneath her, who looks down her nose at people and who treats people differently, depending on who they are. I can spot them a mile off. Even taxi drivers always say, 'I thought you'd be a snob but you're not.' I pride myself on that. I've always taken different people home. I took a Rastafarian once with his little son. He's a single father and he had nowhere to go one Easter so I rescued him. I said, 'Come and have family Easter with us.' He'd never been down to the country in his life. He's certainly not from the same

class as me but he was welcomed and treated just like anyone else.

A few months after I interviewed her, she dumped yet another boyfriend, saying that she was fed up with having to pay for everything. This must have been a new experience.

She's no fool but had absolutely no idea how offensive she sounded as she unconsciously affirmed that the class system is alive and powerful. The bouncers, head waiters and taxi drivers that Tara prides herself on calling her equals are all people who have to work exceptionally long hours to make a decent wage. She, on the other hand, is a self-confessed ex-cocaine addict who squandered thousands of pounds on drugs and has rarely done a full day's work in her life. The fact that I found her little-girl charm both irritating and patronizing possibly reveals that I do have a slight chip on my working-class shoulder. I felt angry both with her and with myself.

Woodrow Wyatt was an unctuous unpleasant snob. He spent lavishly in order to serve rich food and expensive wines to the grand and famous and cut back by travelling economy on planes. In her memoirs, his daughter, Petronella, described how her father ate the airline food clumsily from his plastic tray, spilling most of the contents. He'd read the newspapers and then chuck the pages on to the floor so that people tripped over them. When he was bored, he blew up paper bags and burst them, which made terrified passengers think that a bomb had exploded. In short, he behaved like a vulgarian. Presumably, he saw his behaviour as charmingly eccentric. If he'd ever sat next to a working-class passenger behaving in the same way, he would have sneered at him as a vile proletarian.

In 1999, Lady Astor was taken to an industrial tribunal after sacking her cook. 'She was very demanding,' said Lady Astor. 'She asked if she could have the leftover newspapers because she liked to read, and for the vegetable choppings to make soup.' Asking humbly if one might have old newspapers and vegetable peelings is a new conception of demanding behaviour. Obviously, Lady Astor thinks that servants who want to read are getting a bit above themselves.

The upper classes can be incredibly parsimonious. A friend of mine who worked for a rich aristocrat was given the head of a salmon. She thought it would do for her cat and, at the end of the week, found that her meagre wages had been reduced to pay for the fish head which would otherwise have been thrown in the bin. Another friend worked in a grand house owned by friends of the Mountbattens. It was a very tall house so a lift was installed. My friend's employers let her put the vacuum cleaner in the lift, but she wasn't allowed to travel with it herself and had to climb the endless stairs.

When the personal maid of society hostess Margot Asquith was killed in an accident, friends rang with their commiserations. 'Tragic for Parker,' they all said. 'Yes but damned inconvenient for me,' she snapped. The upper classes are confident enough to say what they really think, even if it makes them look like unfeeling monsters. The late Duchess of Argyll had exactly that attitude when the maid who had worked for her for years became ill. 'It's so boring,' she said, and was greatly irritated when a friend of hers brought her very sick maid some flowers. As far as the Duchess was concerned, the working classes were not allowed to get ill and, if they did, they certainly didn't deserve flowers. I asked her if she felt guilty for having been rich all her life without ever having worked and she said, 'Don't be ridiculous, Lynda.' Whenever she'd finished what she wanted to say on the telephone, she simply put the phone down. As Margaret Sweeney, she was the most beautiful débutante of her year. She married a duke because she was a snob but the money came from her father who was a multimillionaire Scottish textile merchant. The Duchess was brought up to believe that if you were rich, amusing and desirable, you had every right to be utterly selfish. No one pointed out that, in the end, this attitude made you wretchedly lonely and she ended up in a nursing home, unloved by her daughter and with few friends. I went to see her towards the end of her life when she was in hospital. She ordered tea for us both and then screamed at a nurse who brought it in, saying the tray was too small. She treated all the medical staff and, indeed, some of her visitors, including me, as though we were her servants.

When the late Marquess of Bristol knocked down a tramp after speeding through Paris in his Bentley, he got out of his car, walked over to the bleeding tramp and said can-tankerously, 'Look what you've done to my bloody bumper.' I had a similar experience when my car crashed into a Porsche on a blind bend. The upper-crust, furious driver stormed over to me as I sat shattered, concussed and momentarily unable to speak. 'Are you foreign,' he yelled, 'or thick?'

Michael Winner is the film-director-turned-restaurant-critic who expects to be fawned upon by restaurateurs, and if they don't treat him like God, he turns nasty. He prefers them to genuflect as he walks in. He wants the best table in the room. When he books at short notice, he assumes other guests will be moved in order to accommodate him. If he's told the restaurant is full, he makes a scene. He thinks his convenience comes before that of any other customer. He has been known to insist that the tables on either side of the one where he is seated be kept empty. Some restaurateurs who are afraid of him give into his absurd demands and inevitably lose money.

He's one of those self-obsessed people who have developed a condition known as fame-itis which afflicts pop stars, film directors, Princess Margaret, Mark Thatcher and certain members of the theatrical profession. Surrounded by sycophants, they believe that nothing matters but their own comfort, appetites and desires. 'Fame gives you pleasure,' says psychiatrist Anthony Clare, 'like drink or gambling or sex. But it doesn't make you happy.' Often, though, it does make some people extremely unpleasant. They are outraged if their most casual need is not met on demand. Fame doesn't corrupt, it merely allows the natural bullies and mega-lomaniacs to carry on as they've secretly always wanted to. People rarely have the courage to say to the famous, 'You are an unpleasant, spiteful little dictator who deserves a good clout.' Michael Winner would no doubt say he has a great sense of humour but, as was said about John Betjeman, 'He's not good on people he ragged ragging him back.'

Sir John was a great social climber, which infuriated his father. Ernest Betjeman and his brother were manufacturers of household articles for the rich. They both had factories and Ernest Betjeman hoped in vain that his son would take over his business but the young John Betjeman yearned only to be a witty, aesthetic dandy. He was described as a common little boy and, in many ways, the hurt and shame remained with him all his life. His father called him 'a rotten low deceitful snob', adding, 'Yes, I'm in trade and proud of it, I am.' The anguish Betjeman experienced fuelled his poetry, which has such truth and intense feeling. The aristocracy has produced few great writers, actors or artists. Possibly, all that inbred self-assurance blocks the creative juices. Great generals come from the upper classes because, as a race, they are used to giving orders and being obeyed.

Luckily some Fameocrats become nicer with wealth, power, adoration and influence. 'It's so easy to be nice, it's so difficult to be unpleasant,' says movie star Roger Moore but he's a rare human being. He's even devoted to Michael Winner, which I suspect means he truly is a saint. This point of view is anathema to actor Nicol Williamson who has a self-obsession bordering on madness. When I took him to the Ritz, he was told very politely that he couldn't have lunch in the restaurant. This was because there is a formal dress code and he was wearing a muffler and a bomber jacket. He threw a penny at the courteous, charming waiter, sneering, 'Don't spend it all at once,' and stormed out. Several people standing in the foyer witnessed his outburst and later in the day I received an apologetic phone call from the Ritz management. 'It's me who should apologize,' I said, 'for bringing such an ill-bred guest.'

It was a salutary reminder that the rich and famous who behave like prima donnas can sometimes cause trouble for hard-working, innocent people. The waiter behaved with consummate tact and charm and *he* was the cultured gentleman, not the offensive, uncouth actor.

'Prima donna is not an expression that should ever be used about women,' said Margaret Thatcher. 'It so accurately describes men.' I would, however, make an exception for actress Lauren Bacall who, on one occasion, got into a lift with several other people. 'Why is it stopping on all these floors?' she demanded. 'I want the sixth.'

I used to envy the unreserved self-assurance of the upper classes but no longer. Many of them have been brought up in a world where servants treat them with deference and they begin to believe they can do no wrong. This can make them churlish, blinkered and insensitive, as Earl Spencer proves. They don't have to strive like the rest of us so they often underachieve.

If any chap wants to behave like a gentleman he should remember that good manners are *de rigueur* and considering other people's feelings is essential. 'Good manners is the art of making those people easy with whom we converse,' wrote Jonathan Swift. 'Whoever makes the fewest persons uneasy is the best bred in the company.' This theory would categorize many aristocrats as extremely ill bred, including the Marquis of Blandford.

'You're a second-rate man who lives in a second-hand stately,' Jamie Blandford said famously to the once hugely rich Wensley Haydon-Baillie, who was entering into voluntary insolvency. Blandford is a tenth-rate former drug addict who brought ignominy and disgrace to his father. He dissipated his inheritance, scrounged off others, rarely earned an honest penny and suffered the ultimate insult – his girlfriend ditched him for Oliver Tobias who played Joan Collins's lover in *The Stud*. The fact that Jamie Blandford belongs to a family renowned for its inherited land and house but not for its brains, wit or character, appears to make him feel superior to the rest of us. If he'd been born into a middle-class family he perhaps wouldn't have wrecked his life in the way he has.

Jamie Blandford has embraced hedonism with unrivalled passion. He has led a squalid failure of a privileged life but his aristocratic arrogance remains. He believes that, because of who he is, he can behave exactly as he likes. It's an extraordinary assumption considering his track record of drugs and deception. He thinks of himself as a gentleman and yet behaves like a yob. In 1990, at Blenheim Palace, he married Becky Few Brown, known at school as Becky Few Brains. She went to Hampden House near Great Missenden in Buckinghamshire. By Becky's own admission, the only girl who was dimmer than her was David Mellor's ex-mistress Antonia de Sancha. At seventeen she went to Redlynch, a finishing school in the West Country run by a headmaster called the Colonel. The privileged, rich young girls were taught cooking, flower arranging, sewing and how to do dinner parties. It was a school for the daughters of the wealthy upper class who would grow up to be the sleek, alluring wives and mistresses of rich and powerful men. It produced confident, controlling charmers rather then career girls. You needed *élan* not brains.

The girls were taught that the finest qualities in any husband were money, power and a title. They all developed loud carrying voices, which were useful in later life when it came to giving orders to staff. They rarely had more than two 'O' levels but they didn't care. They knew that looks, guile and social skills were what they needed to nab the kind of chap who would bring a triumphant glow to Mummy's heart. Certainly, academic excellence was not deemed important because, on the whole, aristocrats can't bear what they call 'bluestocking' women. The school has now closed which is scarcely surprising. In the days of New Labour, you need to know more than how to fold a napkin and make a perfect *tarte tatin*.

Nevertheless, her attributes enabled Becky to catch a marquis and develop a hauteur all her own. After a five-week honeymoon, the Blandfords came back to a Georgian house on the Blenheim estate. They led the glamorous existences of old-fashioned aristocrats. They attended country house weekends in Scotland and shooting parties in Austria with the European nobility. They went water-skiing on Lake Geneva, heliskiing in Zermatt, lazed on private yachts in the South of France and skied at Verbier. Undeniably, Becky is physically brave. She has skied off piste and raced as a jockey at Newmarket.

Wherever she went when she was married to Jamie Blandford, Becky was treated with deference, called Milady, curtsied to and she took to it as to the manor born. She was frequently extremely rude, although indifferent to the fact. When I went to interview her, she said, 'I would have thought the *Daily Mail* would have sent Nigel Dempster,' clearly thinking that I was a bit fourth division. Her husband's belief that normal rules of behaviour don't apply to him brushed off on her and she became detached from reality. After one storming marital row she drove to London to see girlfriends for lunch. She screeched to a halt outside a Kensington restaurant, double-parked her Renault Turbo, left the hazard lights flashing and blocked the narrow street. When a traffic warden wrote a ticket she fled out swearing, drove round the block and re-parked in exactly the same spot.

The Blandfords are now divorced but were a typical example of a couple who had total confidence about their position in the world, not through their abilities or achievements but through their title and possessions. They are moderately good-looking, quite entertaining and not very bright. If they had been born into a different background they would be Mr and Mrs Average. He would probably be a car mechanic and she would be a kennel maid. Undoubtedly, she is fonder of animals than she is of people, probably because they can be trained to respond instantly to orders and don't answer back.

At the time I met Becky she was living in an estate farmhouse. Her husband had made unpleasant threats towards her and there were times when she would shake uncontrollably. I said that I didn't think she ought to live in such a remote area but she erupted with anger, saying icily, 'It's not for you to tell me what I should or should not do.' She is not as vague as she sometimes appears and there is a shrewdness behind her guileless face. As one of her enemies said, 'It takes a certain concentration to marry the heir to one of the best titles in England.' After her marriage, she posed for pictures *déshabillée* for *Tatler* magazine. In a subsequent infamous row about her marriage breakup, her father-in-law, the Duke of Marlborough, said, 'You're a filthy little scrubber and it's all your fault.' This became public when Becky told her old school friend Annabel Heseltine. It was meant to be a private disclosure but Annabel was writing a profile on Becky and included the offensive remark. When the interview appeared, all hell was let loose and Becky rang Annabel to say, 'What on earth do you think you're doing writing things like that? I was talking to you as a friend.' Annabel said, 'Becky, maybe a friend but always a journalist.' It was a mean, dishonourable thing to do but revealed that upper-class girls do behave like cads.

The Blandfords were close friends of Rupert Deen, the Bertie Wooster of his generation. The old Harrovian devoted his rich life to the pursuit of pleasure and providing lavish hospitality for his friends. His favourite boast was that he would never travel on the tube because he didn't wish to associate with the working classes in case he caught our germs. His two great passions are pheasant and partridge shooting. He did have a brief job in insurance but believes that a gentleman is not put on this earth to work. 'Every third generation of the Deen family has worked,' he said. 'Luckily it's not my turn.' Sadly for him, in 1991 he was officially declared bankrupt owing to his losses at Lloyds. Until then, his social engagements followed a well-ordered pattern as he relentlessly 'did the Season'. In a typical year, he would start in January with a visit to South Africa to stay with his great friend Sir William Pigott Brown. Aristocrats love South Africa because they can live as their ancestors lived in the early part of the last century. It's still possible to have a large live-in staff and a team of gardeners to tend your rich green land. Then he would take a rented chalet with an indoor swimming pool in Gstaad. In the spring, there was the Monaco Grand Prix where he rented a yacht, followed by two weeks in St Tropez. Eventually, he would return to London for the Season beginning with his legendary picnic lunches on the Wednesday of Royal Ascot. For the next couple of months he'd cruise in the Greek Islands and then rent a huge villa in St Tropez for the whole of September. After that he'd drive back in his Mercedes to London, stopping off in Paris for the famous horse race Prix de L'Arc de Triomphe. After a few weeks in London, the pheasant shooting season would start, and he'd stay at various famous stately homes around Britain. He appeared in a Yorkshire Television documentary and was asked why he shot innocent birds. Famously he said, 'All I know is that pheasants are reared to be shot, Labradors are born to retrieve them and Welshmen exist to go down coal mines. Enough of your whingeing.' Around the same time, Lady Elizabeth Shakerley explained how to treat the working classes. 'You must be genuinely interested in whether their chilblains are hurting them,' she said. It's the kind of patronizing remark which makes me want to join the Workers' Revolutionary Party.

The Duke and Duchess of Marlborough live in their sixteen-bedroomed private apartments at Blenheim Palace, described by Jilly Whitehead, their one-time housekeeper, as 'a mansion within a palace'. The Duchess is the daughter of a Swedish aristocrat and is renowned for her autocratic air, sharp temper and belief that servants don't have feelings. 'When a lady guest went down for dinner,' says the housekeeper, 'I would have to go in and tidy her room. The Duchess insisted everything in the bathroom was dried, especially the tub and even the toothbrush. If a guest was sleeping alone, the bed – which was made with linen sheets, three woollen blankets, a silk cover to hide them and a lace throw – had to be turned down diagonally. If she was half of a couple, it would be horizontal. A nightdress and dressing gown would be laid out. Her Grace liked them draped fully across a chair with their arms pulled across the front, never folded in half. She wanted everyone's bedside light turned on, the shutters closed and curtains drawn. I had to put silver flasks of iced water by the bedsides, but Her Grace instructed me to always wipe my fingerprints off them the minute they were in place. A lot of the ladies liked to stay in bed until lunchtime. I had to bring them whatever breakfast they ordered and their favourite newspaper on a wicker tray with special legs. I was once asked to wake one guest every five minutes until she stopped dozing off. She used me like a human snooze button. When the ladies came to leave I would pack for them, wrapping everything in tissue paper. If they had a lot of velvet, which the Duchess insisted was turned inside out for travelling, then it could take a couple of hours.'

The housekeeper was also told that she must only ever say 'Good morning' or 'Good afternoon' to any guests or members of the family. I imagine this was because she was only a servant and anything more fulsome would be deemed personal and therefore impertinent. These are the orders of a duchess who believes that the world is divided into aristocrats and menials. She would not stop to think that her behaviour was rude or offensive and I find this rather chilling. Recently, the family advertised for an under-butler, which is probably Marlborough-speak for servile workhorse.

Entertaining at Blenheim is done in the old-fashioned way. They have regular shooting parties and weekend parties where all the guests dress for dinner. The Duchess is said to desperately want her stepson, Jamie Blandford, to be disinherited in favour of her own son, Edward. Top toffs have natural authority on account of the fact that generations of their family have always been in charge.

Recently, a young Buckingham Palace maid went to help out at the current Duke and Duchess of Gloucester's apartments. One morning, when she was carrying a huge pile of linen, she came across her royal employer. 'Good morning Your Royal Highness,' she said. Before she could take another step the Duchess said, 'Haven't you forgotten something?' The startled maid replied, 'I don't think so, Ma'am.' To which the Duchess replied sharply, 'You didn't curtsy.'

The Gloucesters have an impressive apartment at Kensington Palace. The vast drawing room has a staircase leading down to a private walled garden. There is a butler, under-butler, a cook, chauffeur, two daily maids and an office with two private secretaries. When the Duke and Duchess walk their two King Charles spaniels in Kensington Gardens, they are accompanied by police bodyguards funded, naturally, by the taxpayer. One year, along with the Kents and the Ogilvys, they went to the Chelsea Flower Show. Their cars were flanked by police outriders, and motorists in

Knightsbridge sat fuming as the traffic was stopped for the convenience of this group of minor royals. Two days later, three police outriders accompanied the Duke of Kent's Jaguar as he swept into the courtyard of Buckingham Palace. Prince Charles believes that his relations are making excessive use of the police and royal transport. He would like to downsize the royals and thinks, rightly, that they are increasingly irritating the public.

Surprisingly, Earl Spencer also purports to believe that the aristocracy is a spent force and says that while the world observed the power and wealth his ancestors enjoyed, they did not appreciate the downside of being part of an illustrious family. 'A lot of my forefathers,' he says, 'would rather have been doing other things.' He believes his own children will benefit from an increasingly classless society. This is not convincing from a man who has demonstrated awesome arrogance. He always believes he is right, gives orders and expects to be obeyed. His ex-wife Victoria admitted she was frightened of him and said before they were divorced that 'He was a terrifying, intolerant bully, who never allowed me to have an opinion or a voice.' When she was suffering from anorexia and close to a nervous breakdown, he revealed that his father had told him he should stick with Victoria through thick and thin. 'Well, Victoria is thin,' he said viciously, 'and she's certainly thick.' During the divorce hearing, he was exposed as a cheat, a liar and an adulterer who did everything he could to humiliate and demean his wife. He was later described by his former mistress Chantal Collopy as someone who pursues women but then gets bored and drops them.

Earl Spencer, who despised the commercial instincts of his stepmother, Raine, has turned Althorp into an even more lucrative business. The year after he opened the area devoted to his sister Diana, he sent out unctuous letters to potential customers urging them to visit. Now that it's only open for two months of the year, he is prepared to let the public buy mementoes on the Internet all year round. He explains that he doesn't want them to be disappointed. He lives in an era when only rock stars can afford to live without the paying public and a ticket collector at the gate. The Duke of Bedford had to make Woburn into a tourist attraction, and Longleat with its 9,000 acres is famous more for its lions than its history and ancestors.

The late Earl Spencer was left by his wife Frances when she fell in love with wallpaper manufacturer Peter Shand Kydd. Her husband originally agreed that she should have custody of their four children but bitterness made him vengeful. He chose to fight and his mother-in-law Lady Fermoy was his staunchest ally. She double-crossed her daughter and testified for her son-in-law. She did it because she didn't want her grandchildren to be brought up by a wallpaper manufacturer and, above all, she wanted to protect her royal connections as the royals in those days disapproved of the stigma of divorce. She said that, in her opinion, her daughter was not fit to have custody of her children and Earl Spencer won the case. They would actually have been far happier with their mother and Lady Fermoy's ruthlessness virtually ruined their young lives. She put status before everything and class-consciousness before compassion, loyalty or love.

Fergie's father, Major Ronald Ferguson, was a client of the Wigmore Club, which provided sexual services for rich and powerful men. When this was revealed, he was vilified but, rather than feeling repentant, he was outraged by the furore. 'The Club was a marvellous place to go and be cocooned away,' he told me. 'Like a lot of other men, I personally have felt it necessary to switch off at somewhere like the Wigmore for a couple of hours. It is only because there's a ridiculous hypocritical sexual attitude in this country that anyone made any fuss. But as Sarah had just got married, I suppose I should have had more sense.' I think he should also have had more dignity and self-respect. He believes his own family is superior to the royals although he has had to bear the ignominy of hearing himself continually called 'the disgraced Major Ron'. What is more, his name is spelt with only one 's', which is very un-smart. He prides himself on his breeding and background but behaved in a seedy and reprehensible way. When Major Ron became engaged to farmer's daughter Sue Deptford, who became his second wife, his mother, Lady Elmhirst, began checking on her future daughter-in-law's background. She was appalled because she didn't know Sue's family and Sue hadn't done the season or been a deb. She was obsessed with Sue's lineage rather than pleased that she had a loving heart. There are still mothers who care more about their son's wife's social standing than they do about her character. It's even more proof that the values of the upper classes are not necessarily right, wise or enviable. In the end, Major Ron was shamed and dishonoured by the sexy, lower-middle-class Lesley Player, who entrapped him to further her ambitions. He slept with her in Fergie's house, with his daughter's consent. Sue had been a loving stepmother to Fergie for many years, so this was a pretty grubby, ill-bred way to repay her. When the whole tawdry story emerged, she was almost more upset by her stepdaughter's perfidy than by Major Ron's infidelity. She's the traditional, head-in-the-sand kind of wife who always blames the other woman and not her husband.

Ronald Ferguson was Prince Charles's polo manager for

twenty-one years and his own version of his character is that he's an honourable, shy and decent, well-bred chap who is happiest on his farm. He has described his mother as 'a crashing snob', yet says he has not got a snobbish bone in his body but I'm not convinced. When Lesley Player wrote a book about their furtive affair, the aspect which seemed to upset him most was her inaccurate statement that he wore a blazer at Claridge's. 'A gentleman,' he said, 'would never do that.' He was far more worried about being portrayed as a man who didn't know how to dress correctly than by the fact that he'd been exposed as a lecherous fool. In addition, he'd been made an idiot of by a grasping social climber who duped him. Lesley Player wanted to set up a ladies' international polo tournament and believed his royal connections would be useful to her business aspirations. She pursued him outrageously and he was hooked. 'She just wanted to use me,' said the Major, 'and climb up the tree.' He and his wife were desperately worried about money but that didn't stop him giving his avaricious mistress a polo pony and a ball gown. Certainly, it's difficult to believe a man is shy when he shows you a picture of himself in suspenders and women's underwear at a friend's fortieth birthday party.

So, if you behave like a cad, can you still be called a gentleman? There are those who would say 'Yes', because their definition of a gentleman would depend on class, not behaviour. Personally, I disagree. The characteristics of a gentleman are not only found in one class. Nobs do not have the monopoly on courage, civility, charm and integrity.

7
TRUE CLASS

During my career as a journalist, I've interviewed princesses, miners, prime ministers, movie stars, market traders, dukes, countesses, bus drivers and billionaires. I know beyond any shadow of a doubt that impressive men and women with true class come from all backgrounds. 'University isn't for people like us,' David Blunkett's mother told him. However, ability, pride and cussedness drove him on, despite his blindness. Now he's Secretary of State for Education and holds one of the highest positions in the land. His achievement is awe-inspiring. It's the story of a working-class chap who embodies the finest qualities in human nature. David Blunkett more than anyone reaffirms that good breeding is not dependent on class. Neither injustice nor blindness has ever embittered him. When he was only twelve years old, his father, who was already past retirement age, was still working for the gas works in Sheffield. A colleague failed to repair a safety device, despite being ordered to do so, and Arthur Blunkett fell into a vat of scalding water. He saved himself from drowning by hanging on to the rim by one arm but the rest of his body was horribly scalded. He was taken to Sheffield Royal Infirmary and a month later he died. It was a terrible, shameful incident and the Gas Board behaved with brutal parsimony. They said David's father was over sixty-five so compensation was not appropriate as he was at the end of his working life. 'My mother had a twelve-year-old who couldn't see,' says David Blunkett, 'my very old, frail grandmother was living with us and she was ill herself with breast cancer. There was no money coming in and her husband was dead. It is quite a lot to cope with, isn't it? Even at twelve I remember thinking, "Best if I try and be supportive rather than a burden."'

Nicholas Soames is the grandson of Sir Winston Churchill and a very upper-class gentleman. His father was the British Ambassador to Paris and he went to Eton but he values people for what they are, not who they are. He judges them on their merits, not their superficial grandeur. One of his great heroes is Tony Blair's press secretary Alastair Campbell. 'He's absolutely brilliant,' says Mr Soames. 'He's funny, he's got style, he's light on his feet, he's brave and bloody marvellous at what he does.' In fact, Nicholas Soames admires Mr Campbell so much that he paid him the ultimate upper-class compliment and said, 'I'd go tiger hunting with Campbell any day. Once somebody was criticizing a certain politician to my grandfather. He said, "I wouldn't go tiger hunting with him." Winston said, "Tiger hunting? I wouldn't hunt a mouse round a fucking sofa with him."'

Nicholas is a shoulder-to-the-wheel kind of chap who doesn't like public shows of emotion or what he calls 'blubbing in your tent'. He has exquisite manners and the confidently unique vowel sounds of the upper class. He says 'hice' for 'house' and 'mionaise' for 'mayonnaise'. He adores P. G. Wodehouse and it's very easy to envisage him as a Wodehouse character. 'I would die in a ditch for my friends,' he says, and I am sure he would. He talks about 'good eggs' and 'spiffing girls' and thinks it's his duty to be amusing. He's gloriously and unashamedly politically incorrect. He started hunting at the age of three and shot his first stag at fourteen.

When his daughter Isabella was born, he said she was the size of a decent salmon.

He served in the 11th Hussars and then became equerry to the Prince of Wales. An ex-girlfriend said that being made love to by him was like having a large wardrobe with a very small key falling on top of you. Prince Charles has been a friend since they were schoolboys and was best man at his first wedding. He was one of the few people to counsel Prince Charles against marrying Diana Spencer and was never her fan. Lots of people think he's arrogant, which isn't surprising. When he went to stay with the Duke of Devonshire, his idea of a joke was to say to the left-wing Dennis Skinner, Labour MP for Bolsover, 'Ah, Skinner, I'm coming to your part of the country for the weekend. I'll try to look in at your place for a few oysters.' Mr Soames admits he's not as humble as he might be, saying, 'I always sing that marvellous song, "Oh Lord it's hard to be humble when you're perfect in every way".'

Mr Soames is a bit of a dandy who always looks wonderful and as though he has the daily attentive care of a personal valet. His ankle-length overcoat is a replica of the one worn by Lord Ribblesdale in John Singer Sargent's portrait of him in the National Gallery. 'I was a soldier,' he says, 'and I know it's deeply pompous and stuffy but I like to be properly turned out, with ironed suits and sparkling shoes and creases in your trousers. This idea in politics advanced by Michael Portillo that we're into the era of the rolled-up sleeves and the jacket is nonsense. I don't want my presidents and my prime ministers looking as if they've just climbed off the back of a beach truck.' His late, great friend Alan Clark described Nicholas as having 'a social passport to every grand house in the country'.

People with class rarely complain and have a great capacity for fortitude. They make light of their troubles and think that one has a duty not to burden other people. Sir John Mills personifies the breed with his wit and valour and determination to mask much personal suffering. His dignity, sweetness and courage are humbling. He is almost blind and his wife has Alzheimer's but he believes that, even if your heart is breaking, you put on a smile and give a performance. He is always immaculately dressed and looks as though he's just ready to step on to the musical comedy stage. He calls everyone 'darling' and looks at you with such alert interest it's hard to believe that he can see little more than darkness. 'I've been terribly lucky,' he says, 'so I can't feel sorry for myself, can I? I have my moments but, if I get low, I have a whisky, maybe two. I try not to have three.' Sir John epitomizes Kipling's famous poem and truly does treat triumph and disaster just the same.

Sir Alec Guinness did exactly that, and although the last few years of the great actor's life were often occupied with physical problems, he wrote about them with humour and almost disdain. His friend Keith Baxter said movingly when he died, 'Those of us who were graced with his friendship cherished it and took the utmost pains to see that we never lost it. He despised ostentation, boorishness, unpunctuality and slovenliness. He liked quirkiness, attractive manners and laughter, the good-looking and the odd and letters written in longhand in pen and ink.'

Equally, the brilliant comedian Les Dawson was a true gentleman whose brilliance, wisdom and sense of his own worth meant that he treated everyone in precisely the same way. 'Where's Dawson?' the Duke of Edinburgh used to cry whenever they were at the same dinner. The last interview he gave before he died was to the psychiatrist Anthony Clare. Subsequently, Dr Clare revealed how he had wanted the comedian to meet a group of his patients who were suffering from depression, to talk about his philosophy. The two men shared a belief in the healing power of laughter and the psychiatrist wrote, 'I know that Les would have given them laughter and for a brief moment anyway brought them close to joy.'

Les fulfilled all his childhood fantasies of what constituted glamour. His house in St Anne's near Blackpool had huge black wrought-iron gates with the initials of Les and his wife inscribed in gold. The same initials were emblazoned in gold on the maroon sunblinds at every window. The long hall was lined with statues. In the dining room there were six ornate Italian padded chairs around a flower-painted table which was permanently laid for a formal dinner party. There was a vast, hanging, crystal candelabrum and another gilt candelabrum, lavishly decorated with cherubs, on the sideboard. There was a statue of a gentleman with a violin and a lady with a fan and a pink parasol in the fireplace. The french windows led on to the terrace where two stone lions stood guard. Miniature gnomes peeped out from a bed of ivy next to a statue of a naked lady. The purists would say it was a monument to bad taste but it seemed to me to be a monument to Les's sense of total security. He was at ease in his own skin and could meet stars, royalty, miners and fans and treat them all with courtesy and humour. He grew up in poverty in a northern council house and he wanted glamour, lushness and lashings of gilt with a touch of Versailles. He wanted what *he* wanted, not some interior-designed perfection. 'Not bad for a Manchester lad,' he used to say. 'I just wish my mam and dad were still around to see it.'

The important thing in the end is that we all surround ourselves with the kind of décor which gives us pleasure. Les had the confidence to create the ambience he wanted. Clearly, it was the much-loved house of a working-class lad who had got to the top. If you grow up in bleak poverty, you do yearn for ornate gilt and lushness and swagged velvet curtains. There was nothing minimalist about Les Dawson.

In Les's speech at his wedding to his beautiful second wife, Tracy, he quipped, 'Tracy and I have had a slight disagreement. I've gone to a hell of a lot of trouble to book a caravan for her honeymoon. But now she doesn't want to go. She wants to come to the South of France with me.' In fact, they had a very upper-class honeymoon. They flew in a private plane to a castle surrounded by a moat and a forest on an island in the Scottish Highlands.

Old Harrovian Julian Wilson, who was the BBC's racing commentator, is an old-fashioned top toff. He has an innate conviction that chaps should be brave, loyal and never blub. He's fearless, takes risks, adores beautiful women and believes in the stiff upper lip and never showing emotion, even if your wife or horse dies. If he'd been in the army, he would have ended up a taciturn general who would have fallen on his sword for his men. He says:

My generation believed that a gentleman doesn't show emotion. All those values were embodied in the attitude of the royal family at the late Princess of Wales's funeral. They behaved in the way that you *should* behave, instead of blubbing and leaving mountains of flowers all over London. We grew up believing that we had to set an example and support one another. If there was ever going to be another war you knew the people that you'd be happy to stand in the trenches with. Society has now turned absolutely upside down. It's all about counselling, psychotherapy and emotional stuff which my generation didn't believe in.

His mother's childhood home was a house called Kitemore where the old Berkshire Hunt used to meet. There were stone kites on the gates at the end of the drive and she hunted, did the Season and went to endless dances. Her old nanny brought up Julian and told him, 'A gentleman shouldn't get married until he's twenty-nine.' In the old days, this meant when he was established in his profession, with a sizeable income. When my husband's parents married, my father-in-law was a doctor in the RAF. He was twenty-nine but didn't get a marriage allowance for a year because officers and gentlemen were not expected to marry until they were thirty. There was intense social rigidity in the RAF at the time. An air vice-marshal's wife might invite a squadron leader and his wife to a cocktail party but never to a dinner party. I can see the sense of it because it is easier to take orders from a leader who is not socially a friend.

There is no doubt that people are impressed and influenced by titles. Lady Berkeley is a shrewd realist who is quite prepared to capitalize on her name to make people take notice of her. She is a passionate defender of the environment and says, 'If you have six names on a list complaining about something and one of them has got a title, people listen. It opens doors.' She is absolutely right and it even helps to sell theatre tickets. Boxer Henry Cooper is a seasoned performer who does his own one-man show. He's always been popular but the minute he got his knighthood his bookings doubled. He's a South Londoner from a working-class family. He's brave, honest, fearless, modest and would always stand up and be counted. He has all the qualities which are associated with an officer and a gentleman. His grandfather was a bare-knuckle fighter who every Sunday used to walk twelve miles from London's Elephant and Castle to Blackheath. After the fight he would trudge painfully home and hold out his hands. They were so bruised and bleeding he couldn't take the money he'd earned out of his pocket. His grandson grew up to be one of the best-loved men in Britain. Sir Henry is revered for his boxing talent but also for the fact that neither fame nor honours have ever changed his gentleness, dignity or modesty.

'Do as you would be done by' is a good motto for all gentlemen. Lord Snowdon's late father once lived in a very grand house in Sussex. One Sunday afternoon, some people drove up the drive and began to picnic on his land. Ronald Armstrong Jones went up them and said, 'Good morning. Good morning. I live here. This is my house but I'm delighted you're having a picnic. I just hope when you depart you won't leave any rubbish.' The man was very rude and, when they finally went, they left sandwich wrappings and other litter. Ronald Armstrong Jones plotted his revenge and managed to find out where the trespassers lived. He put two deckchairs and a hamper from Fortnum's in the boot of his Daimler. He then drove over to the man's house with his wife. When they arrived they got out of the car, put up the deckchairs on the front lawn and opened the hamper. The man came out shouting, 'What do you think you're doing?' Mr Armstrong Jones said, 'We're having a picnic here just as you did last Sunday on my land. The only difference is that we won't leave any rubbish.'

Aristocrats have a far greater sense of duty than most of us.

Princess Alice, Duchess of Gloucester, was the daughter of the Duke of Buccleuch. She nearly drowned when she was a young girl. Before she was saved she prayed, 'Oh God, give me life. I promise I'll make use of it if you'll give it back to me.' She kept the promise and twenty years later she accepted the proposal of King George V's dull, dour, shy son Prince Harry because she felt it was her duty. It was a difficult marriage since he was a heavy drinker and, when she was widowed and in her eighties, she lost her beloved family home, Barnwell Manor. Her son, the Duke of Gloucester, was unable to afford the upkeep and it has now had to be rented out.

When Princess Alice was a child, the Buccleuch family had their own state coach and their own railway train. Every few months, the servants, horses, children and luggage would be loaded on to the train and they would move on to one of their ancestral homes, which included Eildon Hall in Roxburgh-shire and Drumlanrig Castle in Dumfriesshire. 'How extraordinary, Ma'am,' I said when I met her at Kensington Palace, 'to have your own railway train.' She looked at me in surprise and made an enviably smart riposte. 'Oh in those days,' she said, 'everybody did.'

Wynne Johnson is the mother of Lee Clegg who served with the army in Northern Ireland. When he was on duty one evening in September 1990, he and his colleagues fired at a stolen car which crashed through a checkpoint. A young girl died and Lee was charged with murder. He was convicted and sent to Wakefield Prison. There was a time when Wynne was intimidated by so-called important people but no longer. She has seen the perfidy, treachery and cowardice of many of them. In the early days of her campaign, she was patronized, told not to make waves and to let the army look after Lee. If she had capitulated, Lee would still be in prison. She is a working-class woman who left school at fourteen but she is proud and indomitable with a strong sense of justice. Painfully, as Wynne battled to free her son, she discovered that people in high places with grand titles are not necessarily worthy of admiration or trust. She took on the army and the High Court judges and, in the end, she won. Ultimately, Lee was cleared of murdering Karen Reilly and Wynne said, 'We would have fought for however long it took to get justice. We'd have fought till we died.'

I've never met a powerful, self-made man yet who didn't have an extraordinary capacity for hard work and the ability to exist on five hours' sleep a night. Class doesn't deter working-class highflyers. History is littered with men and women who appeared to have everything and threw it all away. It is also crammed with those who began with nothing and became billionaires. Sir Alan Sugar was born in London's East End and started his first business selling car aerials from the boot of his car. One of his grandfathers migrated from Poland in the 1890s to escape anti-Semitism. The other grandfather was born in Mile End, Stepney, when it was one of the most deprived areas of Britain. Sir Alan made his fortune in the electronics world by supplying simplified gadgets to the masses. He has been trading for as long as he can remember. At thirteen, he was selling boiled beetroots for a local greengrocer and now he is worth £300m.

In 1988, Alan Sugar was judged to be the fifteenth-richest person in Britain but being knighted was the proudest moment of his life. Undoubtedly, honours and titles mean more to men than they do to women. Men want recognition, acclaim and, above all, respect. 'My inspiration,' says Alan Sugar, 'came from trying to break out of the situation my family was in. The system was to leave school at fifteen and get a job in a factory. My father, Nathan, worked as a tailor in a garment factory in the East End. He made £11 a week and he never knew if he had a job to go to the following Monday.'

Actress Barbara Knox, who plays Rita in *Coronation Street*, comes from a working-class background in Saddleworth near the Lancashire moors. 'My parents were real workers who gave me wonderful strengths, a sense of decency and integrity,' she says. 'We were poor but my mother would do without so I could look smart. She worked in the mill but she didn't want it for me. She taught me to have pride, the right sort of pride that means worries are private. We weren't slackwoven, as my aunt used to say. Today, people moan about being poor but my mother would have scrubbed steps to look after me.'

One of the most top-class people I have ever met is Dame Cicely Saunders. She is a middle-class girl who was educated at Roedean. She trained as a nurse and, in her late thirties, she qualified as a doctor. She is the inspirational, dynamic woman who created the modern hospice and her ideas about the best way to die have been copied all over the world. She has taken the fear out of dying for so many people and, in 1967, she founded St Christopher's at Sydenham, South London. It's a vibrant, enriching place with views over the garden and vivid collages, tapestries and paintings on the wall. There is a feeling, not of finality or defeat, but of energy and optimism. Wine is served with lunch and Dame Cicely is partial to a stiff whisky. It took her nineteen years to find the site of St Christopher's and she wrote literally 10,000 letters in the Herculean task of raising the money. Terminally ill patients are encouraged to say what is in their hearts and do what they want to do. The family is incorporated into the process and helped to speak of their truest feelings so that, when the end comes, there are no regrets over things left unsaid.

Dr Shaun Russell became high profile through tragedy but he coped with selfless courage. His wife, Lin, and daughter, Megan, were murdered as they walked home from school and his elder daughter, Josie, was left for dead in a pool of blood. Dr Russell behaved at all times with gentlemanly civility to the media. He gave up his own career to look after Josie and took her to live in a remote Welsh cottage where the healing powers of the mountains have worked their magic. Against all the odds, Josie has turned into a healthy, confident, glowing beauty. This is due to her own strength of character but also to her father's devotion and commitment.

Richard Burton retained his mellifluous Welsh accent when he needed it and played the boy-from-the-valleys role but he could also sound like an English toff. He first met Elizabeth Taylor during a Californian swimming party at a glamorous house in Bel Air and he was astounded and rather shocked by her blasphemous language. In what he always called his 'best chiffon and cut-glass accent', he said, 'You have a remarkable command of Olde English.' When she asked him if they didn't use words like that at the Old Vic, he said, 'They do but I don't. I come from a family and an attitude that believe such words are an indication of weakness in vocabulary and emptiness of mind.'

Richard had a rare ability to move effortlessly through every class. He was at home anywhere and so were his brothers and sisters. They possessed a natural inner confidence and treated everyone with gentle politeness. They were never in awe of the grand and great and, equally, they never felt superior. They were simply themselves wherever they went. They had innate good breeding and Richard's fellow countryman Simon Weston has precisely the same qualities. He was so savagely burnt in the Falklands War when the *Sir Galahad* was bombed that 80 per cent of his body is grafted tissue. He was in and out of hospital for years and experienced both pain and despair but he determined to remake his life. He founded the Weston Spirit which helps the most vulnerable inner-city teenagers who are trapped in empty, sad lives. He helps them to find something they have never had which is self-respect. 'The most important thing if you do become injured,' he says, 'is how you cope. If you spend your life full of recriminations and bitterness, then you've failed yourself, failed the surgeons and nurses and everyone else because you aren't giving anything back. Hate can consume you and it's a wasted emotion. I say to the boys and girls in Weston Spirit, "Make a difference even if it's only to your own life."'

'Simon does have this knack of touching people emotionally,' says his wife Lucy. 'He doesn't set out in the morning to say, "I'm going to make people feel better." It's just something he's got, it's in him. People go away from him feeling they have something they didn't have before.' Simon Weston's army career was spent in a class-conscious environment in which he was the lowest of the low but he has the ability to meet kings and commoners and treat them all with grace.

Again and again, men to whom I have talked, young and old, rich and poor, from all classes, have used the phrase 'The kind of chap you'd be glad to have in the trenches with you.' It's their idea of the ultimate compliment. They mean a man who never makes an unnecessary fuss, doesn't use five words when two will do, quietly does what has to be done, never panics and is not primarily concerned with his own skin. It is not a phrase that women use, but if ever I were in a trench, I'd certainly like Dame Cicely and Wynne Johnson next to me. I wouldn't want Prince Charles, the Marquis of Blandford or Tara Palmer Tomkinson.

ARE YOU SOCIALLY CONFIDENT?

Yes No

1 If you didn't understand the meaning of 'La roulade de loup farci aux morilles et asperges', would you have the courage to ask the waiter to explain?

2 Do you feel at ease with people irrespective of their background?

3 Can you cope with eating artichokes at a dinner party?

4 If you were seated on your host's left rather than his right, would you be amazed?

5 Can you eat canapés at one go rather than biting off bits and spilling crumbs down your front?

6 Do you think it's absurd to surreptitiously wipe your lipstick off your wine glass in the hope that people won't see?

7 If you tripped over as you walked into a restaurant, would you merely laugh?

8 Can you complain without going bright red? ☐ ☐

9 At a party, are you happy to introduce
   yourself to other guests? ☐ ☐

10 Do you find it simple to extricate yourself
    from a conversation? ☐ ☐

If you answered 'yes' to more than 7 of these questions, you
   are pretty suave.
If you answered 'yes' to 4–6 of these questions, you've got
   panache.
If you answered 'yes' to less than 4, you're a social lump.

8

CHANGING CLASS

In many ways, moving from one class to another is a bit like moving from an outdated computer to the latest, intimidating, high-tech one. I've recently moved from an obsolete, reliable, sunny-tempered, easy machine on to one which almost thinks for me. It's so smart that it's usually a sentence or two ahead and is forever giving me instructions, telling me off or issuing warnings. For months, I had both machines on my desk. Whenever the new one made me too fraught, I went back to the old one which was always a comfort. Gradually, the smart one took over and finally won. My original machine was taken away and, in the end, I didn't even miss it. In a similar way, once you have totally moved away from one class you can't really go back.

Two years ago, I met an old school friend I hadn't seen for over three decades. In our youth, we'd shared confidences, hopes and dreams and I was so looking forward to seeing her again but it was a disaster. Sadly, we'd become strangers and it was a relief to both of us when we parted never, I'm sure, to meet again.

There are times in the early stages of changing class when you regret the warm, cosy security of a world you know, but in the end it seems too confining, claustrophobic and narrow. I wouldn't want to go back to living on a Lancashire council estate although I still love chips and potato cakes. So, if you want to change your class, what should you do?

Despite the fact that this is screamingly politically incorrect advice, you should first lose your regional accent whether it be Lancashire, Cornish or West Country. If you have a good ear, this shouldn't be a problem but it will involve speaking slowly for quite a long time. Sue Lawley now has what we used to call a cut-glass accent. It's a long time since she was a working-class student in the Black Country standing at a bus stop saying, 'Coom on boos.' Her father did his own milk round and her mother ran a shop in the West Midlands. Sue went to Dudley Girls' High School and then to Bristol University. She shared digs with an upper-crust girl and decided to remake herself. A posh voice is still an asset, particularly if you want to complain or book a table in a restaurant. When asked how to get a table at London's Ivy, Clarissa Dickson Wright made it clear that sounding assured invariably does the trick. 'Start with your name,' she said, 'as if they should recognize it. If they demur ask to speak to their superior. Do not be rude, just assertive and remember the old adage: "Persistence and perseverance made a bishop of his reverence."'

A posh voice is like a carapace, which is something comedian Kenneth Williams realized. He was born into a working-class family in the Caledonian Road in London in 1926. He was brilliant and arrogant but always felt a misfit. He had an acutely accurate ear for dialects, and whenever he felt uneasy or threatened, he hid behind his famously exaggerated upper-class vowels. I do the same myself, and whenever I'm nervous, sound posher by the minute.

Lord Lichfield, who has a naturally upper-crust voice, had affairs with Britt Ekland and Bianca Jagger. He says grandly that if either of them had come from a farm in Gloucestershire, 'It is perfectly possible I might have married one of them.' He means that if either of them had been the débutante daughter of a wealthy aristocratic landowner he'd have thought they were good enough for him. Clearly, he assumes that if he had wanted to get married, both beauties would have jumped at the chance. Patrick Lichfield lost his virginity when he was very young to his twenty-six-year-old art teacher. In her seventies, she's still alive, and he says, 'I suppose she was my Mrs Robinson.' In the end, he reverted to type and married Lady Leonora, sister of the Duke of Westminster, whose family own 300 acres of Mayfair and Belgravia. Understandably, she left him. They divorced in 1986 after eleven years of marriage and his amour is now Lady Annunziata Asquith.

If you belong to the kind of family which thinks it's a sin to get above yourself, then the only solution is to leave home. This is what theatre director Sir Peter Hall did although his parents adored and believed in him. 'I was the cliché,' he says, 'an only child, the scholarship boy, the working-class lad who turned himself into a phoney member of the middle classes. I was not as generous or grateful to them as I should have been.'

He regrets his old feelings, which were possibly an amalgam of irritation and shame, and says, 'I think I was a bad son. My mother was always saying, "We haven't heard from you, you haven't been to see us, are you alive?" She made demands on me, she was exhausting. I spent many years not liking her. I owe a tremendous amount to her ambition, protectiveness and encouragement. She fought my battles. She was one of those people to whom love means possession. I suppose I was her great love. Everything she wanted for herself she put into me. But everything that was done for me, from going from elementary school to grammar school to university, made it more impossible for me to connect with my family. In the end, we had nothing to talk about.'

His mother's ambition and the sacrifices she made for her brilliant son meant that, to a certain extent, she lost him. Sometimes, sons and daughters have to leave home before they can change. Indeed, you can't practise a new accent if you are constantly being ridiculed. This was never a problem for me as my mother yearned for me to have an upper-class voice. Pronunciation was sometimes difficult, as Joe Lampton in John Braine's novel *Room at the Top*, found when he said 'brazier' instead of 'brassière'. Even these days, if I'm nervous, I can sound, at best, unnaturally stilted and, at worst, overexcited. This is not helped by the fact that the one residue of my youth that I have never been able to overcome is an unfortunate tendency to turn bright red when I'm feeling uneasy.

If you are committed to changing your voice, don't worry about the fact that one day you will be exposed as an impostor or a phoney. Once you have established yourself as urbane, sophisticated and socially acceptable, people are intrigued to hear about an Eliza Doolittle background.

Paul McCartney's new lady is Heather Mills, who lost part of her leg in a motorbike accident. She is a classic case of a working-class girl who moved onwards and upwards. She was born in Newcastle, began work as a teenage cocktail waitress and ultimately lost her Geordie accent. Novelist Beryl Bainbridge took elocution lessons to ditch her Liverpool twang. Will Carling's wife, Liza, is a steelworker's daughter from Sheffield. She grew up in a council house but has the fine, chiselled features and autocratic vowel sounds of a Home Counties ex-deb. When she first came to London, she changed her name from Wolk to Deveraux. She told me this was because Wolk was difficult for people to understand when she said it on the telephone. I can think of a lot of simple, short, easily pronounced names, but Deveraux isn't one of them. I suspect the real truth was that she wanted to sound posher and more interesting than the child of a working-class Polish immigrant from Sheffield – and why not? If people then believed she was the indulged daughter of a French aristocrat it didn't do her any harm.

Now Liza is elegant and confident and her metamorphosis is complete. Ultimately, the truth about her background came out, as it always does, but her husband finds her working-class origins rather endearing. Whether her in-laws, who are ex-army, feel the same way is not on record. Army officers spend their lives in a rigid, cast-iron social structure so they would possibly feel happier if their high-profile son had married a girl from their own world. On the other hand, his first wife, Julia, was middle class but she loathed her in-laws and they detested her.

Having changed your accent, the next step is to change your vocabulary. If you can become best friends with a girl or chap who is socially impeccable, this is a good start. Hopefully, they will invite you to their parents' house and you will be able to pick up a lot of tips. This is what I did, having become friends at drama school with an incredibly glamorous fellow student called Heather. Her parents lived in a mansion near Bristol and, eventually, she became my elder daughter's godmother. We shared a London flat in Eccleston Square and I owe her a huge debt of gratitude.

After my mother, Heather was one of the most influential figures in my life. We've lost touch completely and I would love to see her again but I was always fonder of her than she was of me. She was very sharp when it came to correcting my

pronunciation and I remember my feelings of embarrassment, shame and humiliation to this day. However, I was
anxious to learn and I listened to every word. She mocked me
when I called her parents' drawing room the 'lounge', a bowl
a 'dish', and the lavatory the 'toilet'.

Heather also warned me that it was vulgar to say, 'Pleased
to meet you,' and told me to talk about scent rather than
perfume. I recalled this recently when I went into a large
London store and the assistant on the cosmetics counter said,
'I feel quite undressed without my fragrance.' I still had
trouble with my 'A's, and when I tried to talk posh and
pronounced her sister Anna's name to rhyme with banana,
she laughed with derision. She told me to stop saying
'pardon' when I didn't hear and never in apology. She was
the most stylish person I have ever known and I was utterly
influenced by her clothes and elegance. She was a fanatical
perfectionist, particularly about quality.

I found out that it was rather frightful to cut tomatoes to
look like water lilies and I was staggered to learn that rice
could be used in other ways than rice pudding. Unfortunately, I didn't realize that there were different kinds of
rice, so the first time I made risotto, I used pudding rice and it
turned into mush. Her world of dinner parties was an
absolute eye-opener, since at home, dinner was what we had
at midday and supper was a cup of Ovaltine with a digestive
biscuit just before bedtime. She was so contemptuous about
the naffness of prawn cocktails, tinned fruit, bacon
sandwiches, trifle and custard that I have never eaten them
since. However, I may rethink trifle, having recently
discovered that Sally Clarke of London's famous restaurant
Clarke's makes one with 'gently poached soft fruit and fresh
custard flecked with Madagascan vanilla'. Perhaps I still want

to do the so-called right thing more than I care to believe.

Thanks to Heather, I discovered a whole new way of life and a wholly different kind of food. I tasted for the first time stuffed peppers, moussaka and Stilton. I had my first glass of champagne and instantly loved it. Playwright John Osborne felt the same way and once said to me, 'I drink champagne as you do because we're both upstarts.' I thought it was a lovely word and I still think of myself as an upstart. Years later, I interviewed the great man over lunch. We shared a bottle of champagne and then he chose Château Léoville Barton 1981 at £79 a bottle to go with his roast partridge. Later, we had more champagne and I have absolutely no recollection of how I got home. He came from a lower-middle-class background but was a naturally upper-class person. His houses were always wonderfully stylish with brilliant paintings and he had an instinctive eye for quality. He also had a kind of aristocratic fearlessness when it came to saying exactly what he thought, even if it was vicious and nasty. He excoriated his mother, his ex-wife Jill Bennett (whom he called Hitler) and his daughter, who was his only child. Having moved into an upper-class life by virtue of his talent, he never forgave his daughter for having modest aspirations and I rather sympathized with him. We all want our children to go forwards not backwards. John Osborne and his daughter had a final quarrel when she was sixteen. He ordered her to leave his house and he never saw her again. 'She grew up in a gilded cage,' he said to me once, 'and all she yearned for was a kind of lower-middle-class life. She'd look at houses on new estates and say, "Oh, aren't they nice?" She used to come into my room sometimes in the evenings and I would always take my ring off just in case I couldn't help myself and hit her. Thank God I never did.'

I shared John Osborne's love for a grand lifestyle. I wanted a huge drawing room overlooking my own land and, hopefully, a winding river. I wanted to sit on a terrace having a gin and bianco in the early evening before dinner. I no longer wanted to sit down at six to a 'cooked tea', which might have been egg and chips or what we called 'plate potato pie' with pickled red cabbage. I wanted to belong to a family which held cocktail parties, not hotpot suppers, and invited people to dinner parties. In fact, for a while, I was an unutterable, pretentious, critical, jumped-up little snob who thought she knew it all. I deserved a good slap but it was a tricky phase when I just wanted to discard everything about my old life. I wanted to slough off my working-class skin and adopt an entirely new persona. I yearned to be called Annabel or Sophia.

If you bear any similarity to the old ghastly me – but hopefully with a bit more sense and compassion – then it's useful to learn a bit about art and design. The only picture we had at home in our sitting room when I was a child was a calendar which hung on the wall. It was never opened and the cover picture was of a bluebell wood. However, my mother, who had terrific flair, always made the house look warm and inviting. When other houses in the neighbourhood just had one stark overhead light, we had lamps casting a flattering glow.

I know some upper-class people with appalling taste but because they have inherited family portraits, pictures and good furniture over the years, they are saved from making terrible errors. When Noel Edmonds and his wife moved into their mansion in Devon, they decided to begin their own portrait collection and grand paintings of the Edmondses and their children, looking very stately-homeish, are on the drawing-room walls.

Nouveaux tend to do what they damned well like. One of

the richest men in England is Dave West from Romford who moved to Calais when he realized that the new duty-free laws could make him a fortune. He now owns a chain of drink warehouses called Eastenders and, every week, thousands of people go over from England, Wales and Scotland to stock up. Dave is worth more than £100m but the only concession he's made to changing his class is to buy shoes at £500 a pair in Bond Street. He's left his wife of over thirty years and has a young girlfriend. 'I know why she's with me,' he says bluntly, 'and she knows why she's with me. I'm a market trader pure and simple. People tell me that I should get my accent sorted out and tone things down a bit but I tell them to piss off. I'm not going to change for any toff. And I don't need to. You don't have to be in this game for long to know that the colour of my money is as good as anyone else's.' He is, of course, absolutely right. If you are rich and confident enough, almost all doors open in the end. This is one huge social change that has occurred in the last two decades. There was a time when people like Dave, with his market trader's voice and market trader's cheek, would have been an object of derision. Now, with so many upper-class sons desperately looking for jobs, he may well find that he's courted as a potential employer. Despite his success, Dave regrets his lack of education saying, 'I'm streetwise but I'm uneducated. That has held me back, I'm sure. I can't help but wonder what I would have become if I'd had a few "O" levels to my name.' He probably would not have become a millionaire because his greatest asset is the fact that he comes from a family of market traders. He was helping out on a stall when he was only six and he has an instinctive patter and *chutzpah* which have been of far more use to him than a clutch of 'O' levels. It's a bit like the Somerset Maugham story where the verger is sacked because he can't read. He walks down the street and tries to find a tobacconist to buy a calming packet of cigarettes. He can't see one so, spotting a gap in the market, he uses his redundancy money to open a tobacconist shop. He is so successful that within a few years he owns a chain of shops and is exceedingly rich. When he tells his bank manager that he can't read or write, the banker is amazed. 'You're illiterate and you're so successful,' he says, 'just imagine what you might have achieved and become if you could read and write.' The old man looks at him and says, 'I know exactly what I would be, I'd be a verger.'

Nouveaux have generally worked long and hard for their money but are quite prepared to spend some of it on buying their entrée into the social world of what they call 'the local gentry'. The nobs then eat them out of house and home while turning up their noses at the décor and barking, 'Well done, well done,' when mine host shows off his coach lamps. He got these from a scrap-metal friend who installed them round the kidney-shaped swimming pool which has his name inscribed in the turquoise mosaic.

Footballer and movie star Vinnie Jones, who is very *nouveau*, even had his surname spelt out in ornamental bricks in his drive. The house of a *nouveau* is often newly built because he thinks old houses are full of germs. He insists on having what he calls a patio, which gets floodlit for parties and is very Fergie and Andrew. Fergie is terribly *nouveau* with her belief that if you have it, get some more, preferably without paying for it. 'Clock the rocks,' she said to her friends when she first wore royal jewels. I wrote that she and Andrew had the tastes of a plumber from a council estate in Essex and masses of outraged plumbers' wives from Essex then wrote to complain. They said that they found it hugely insulting to be told they had similar tastes to Fergie. Trying to be ingratiating, I said to a plumber, 'Plumbers are as important as doctors.' He quickly put me in my place by saying, 'Personally, I think we're more important,' and, since water was at that very moment cascading through my ceiling, I could only agree.

The *nouveaux* can't stand a weed or a daisy so their grass looks like a bowling green edged in dreadful French marigolds. This may change now it has emerged that men with lawns which are mown into vertical stripes don't have too much of a sex drive. *Nouveaux* are prone to boasting about their libidos. In fact, when magician Paul Daniels was writing his autobiography, he said he began counting the number of women he'd had sex with but gave up when he got to 300. Since, by his own admission, many of them were one-night stands, I would be amazed if he could recall their faces let alone their names.

Looks are a powerful help to the upwardly mobile, and as far as the late actor Charles Gray was concerned, they provided the basis for his entire career. He was born and raised in suburban Bournemouth and was the son of a surveyor. However, he was tall with aquiline, aristocratic features, a rather supercilious air and the plummy vowels of a toff. He looked what he wasn't and spent most of his professional career playing upper-class baddies.

There are, of course, working-class boys who feel so alienated by their backgrounds that they have no problem with assimilating an upper-class lifestyle. Rock star Bryan Ferry grew up in the pit village of Washington, County Durham, where his father looked after the ponies at the local pit. His house was a back-to-back with a tin bath hanging inside the door and an outside lavatory. He came to London and began to mix with the British upper classes and felt more at ease than he ever had at home. He liked their houses and their décor. He was a huge success in his own right so he didn't feel demeaned or threatened by them. Ultimately, he married his upper-class wife Lucy Helmore, who was brought up in a large house in Campden Hill, in London's Kensington. Later, Bryan Ferry bought the house off Lucy's mother. They also have a house in the country and employ gardeners, maids and nannies. He called their four sons Otis, Merlin, Tara and Isaac and sent them to boarding school. He is irritated by any suggestion that he's a *faux* country squire who has betrayed his roots and I'm on his side. He saw a lifestyle which was infinitely more desirable than the one he'd left and he made enough money to be able to afford it. Tin baths are only romantic when they are part of your past. Now that he's older and the gap between his childhood and his current life is greater, he's become more attached to his roots. It's easy to feel sentimental about the past when there is no danger of having to go back to it.

Bill Wyman is another rock star who detested the squalor of his childhood. He was the eldest of six children and always knew he wanted something better. He shared a bed and bedbugs with his two brothers, and their playgrounds were the bombsites of south-east London. He was the first child in his street to go to grammar school and angered his father who thought he was getting too big for his boots by trying to speak properly. Now he's written a book about the French painter Chagall, has a manor house, Gedding Hall, in Suffolk and a house in Chelsea.

A feeling of alienation is common to those who move from one class to another. Maybe it's the root of aristocratic arrogance, because for generations their families have remained constant in speech, confidence, attitude and even house. The same applies to some working-class families so, possibly, this is why the two classes have traditionally got on so well. They both have a rock-solid base which is why parents often feel threatened when children make it clear they have higher aspirations. The young Alan Bennett was entranced by stories of pipe-smoking fathers and gentle mothers who were invariably referred to as Mummy and Daddy. He made an attempt to substitute these words for his more customary Mam and Dad but was instantly discouraged. 'My father,' he wrote, 'was hot on anything smacking of social pretension.' My mother was exactly the opposite and, like me, was a total convert to social pretension.

John Prescott, on the other hand, having been promoted beyond his ability, appears to uneasily straddle two worlds and not feel quite at home in either of them. When he said that he feels middle class these days, his father vilified him but, of course, John Prescott *is* middle class with his large turreted house in Hull, two Jags, a chauffeur and the deputy leader's grand Admiralty flat overlooking Horse Guards Parade. His father's vituperation is surely based mostly on anger since he is not invited to share his son's powerful, heady new world. This is scarcely surprising because Mr Prescott senior was a vain, egotistical father who left the family home and five children when John was young. Famous sons or daughters who totally reject their parents when they achieve power, wealth and glory usually have good reasons. Those who had loving, supportive parents become even more grateful as they grow older. The ones who felt ignored, abandoned or badly treated by their parents often become more bitter and intransigent. John Prescott has admitted that, despite his formidable achievements, a terrible sense of inadequacy and fear has overshadowed his life. He didn't say he was middle class because he was ashamed of his upbringing. He said it because he was trying to be honest. Having moved from one class to another seems to be at the root of his insecurity. 'I'm so middle class,' he quipped on a television chat show, 'I no longer keep coal in the bath. I keep it in the bidet.' He then roared with laughter although there was bitterness beneath the quip.

Inverted snobs are very quick with phrases like 'Well, we *are* getting above ourselves, aren't we?' or ''Ark at 'er,' as we used to say in Lancashire if anyone made a conscious effort to sound their 'H's. I was laughed at by my contemporaries when I was trying to talk posh and later by my peers because I got it wrong. Even today, I could never get away with talking like the upper-class Candida Lycett Green who once said, 'If I'm feeling low I slip off to the nursery down the road and buy an auricula.' It sounded such a smart remark and I was overcome with envy.

Inverted snobbery can be vicious, condemnatory and divisive. It may well isolate people who want to move up or on. It can humiliate and demean them and many ambitious, clever, working-class students have felt like outcasts. Alison McCullough is a punk and a miner's daughter from Castleford, West Yorkshire, who won a place at St Peter's College, Oxford. At school, she was bullied by her contemporaries because she was clever and liked to work. She was made to feel odd and was called a freak. 'Castleford is a small place,' she says, 'and many of my friends had no ambition to leave there. They just wanted to get married and have children. Then the cycle begins again. I don't blame them though, I simply wanted something else. But at times it was tempting to give it all up, just to be accepted.'

Alison didn't give up, and when she got to Oxford she at

last felt at ease. The granddaughter of sculptor Henry Moore became her best friend. Brains and ability are great levellers and diminish class differences more than anything. 'At Oxford,' she said, 'it was great being able to talk to people who really understood what I was saying about literature, art and music. Back home, I was always having to watch what I said because no one could relate to me at all. I'm sure there were other girls who were just as clever but they weren't prepared to put their heads above the parapet. It takes courage to do that. It's easier to stay in familiar surroundings and not push against the barriers.'

If you truly want to ditch your background, you may have to be utterly ruthless and ditch your parents. Evelyn Waugh did exactly that and never made any bones about wanting to advance himself.

Evidently, John Betjeman displayed the same ruthlessness and few of his friends were ever allowed to meet his father. Many aristocrats have frightful parents. However, although they may detest them, they are never embarrassed by them in the way that people lower down the social scale are ashamed of their relations. I hope my three children aren't ashamed of me although I know I can be a bit embarrassing at times. 'Whenever you're in a hole,' says my son, 'you keep digging,' which is absolutely true. One of the most enviable characteristics of the upper classes is that they never feel the need to explain, elaborate or apologize, which are three things I seem to be continually doing.

Comedienne Rhona Cameron's father was a security guard and she says, 'I know I'm working class because I dress up to visit my bank manager. Middle-class people are much more confident. They wear whatever they want. The class system is all to do with confidence.'

Dedicated class-jumpers need to be calculating because they have to discard not only people, tastes and possessions but sometimes even political allegiance. My mother once went through a phase when she was rather impressed by some smart friends and they persuaded her to vote Tory after a lifetime's allegiance to Labour. She went into the voting booth but, just as she was about to put her cross on the ballot paper, she says she felt she could hear her late father's voice saying, 'Have you gone daft our Peggy?'

I've discarded a lot of things and picked up many superior tastes along the way. Certainly, there must be something about jumped-up working-class girls and sofas. Sue Townsend has eleven in her house and I've lost count of mine. 'The drawing room,' said my daughter, 'looks like Sofa World.'

ARE YOU ONLY PRETENDING TO BE POSH?

	Yes	No
1 Does your accent slip when you lose your temper?	☐	☐
2 Can your family tell who you're talking to on the telephone by the voice you use?	☐	☐
3 Would you tip more generously if people could see the amount?	☐	☐
4 Do you wear bedroom slippers in the kitchen?	☐	☐

5 Do you look sluttish if you're not expecting anyone to call? ☐ ☐

6 Do you wear the old school tie of a posh school you didn't go to? ☐ ☐

7 Do you say to guests, 'Do come and see round the grounds'? ☐ ☐

8 Do you call people 'squire'? ☐ ☐

9 Do you keep the front room for best? ☐ ☐

10 Do you read theatre reviews so that you can pretend you've seen the show? ☐ ☐

If you answered 'yes' to 8 or more of these questions, you're a phoney.

If you answered 'yes' to more than 3 of these questions, you're trying too hard.

If you answered 'yes' to less than 3, you're not convinced you will ever be posh.

9

ENTERTAINING

The way people entertain depends on both money and class. House parties are dependent on the affluence of the hosts and whether or not they can afford staff. In fact, servants can be exceptionally snobbish. When actress Elizabeth Harris became the fourth wife of movie star Rex Harrison, she once picked up a plum from a large bowl in the centre of the dining-room table which had been laid for dinner. The butler came in, slapped her hand and said in total horror, 'Madam those are the master's plums.'

Any socially ambitious hostess inviting several people to stay for the weekend would be shattered by Sunday evening unless she had at least a skeleton staff. Domestic servants are now in short supply, unlike the 1930s when there were 1.4 million in the UK. However, they still exist, and when Tory MP Michael Colvin died in February 2000, he left legacies to fifteen employees including the butler, cook and laundress.

But, apart from the truly grand houses, domestic help may now consist of a daily, the gardener's wife making a few extra pounds and a local, freelance cook. Some hostesses who have known grander days still pretend that all their hard work has been done by unseen staff. So after marinating the pheasant for a Saturday dinner party, she nips upstairs to turn down all the beds and switch on the bedside lamps. She then implies that the hired help did everything. It might seem absurd but we all have our ways of coping and hers is to cry, 'Standards aren't going to drop while I'm still around.' In many ways, she embodies both the strengths and the absurdities of the upper classes. She truly does make one wonder how the British ever lost India.

The upper classes are still addicted to country weekends, which are torture for me as, being *nouveau*, I prefer hotels and room service to private mansions. The late Lord Arran adored staying with other people but couldn't bear having them to stay with him. I'm exactly the opposite and feel totally trapped in a strange house. 'Weekending, by its complex nature,' says one social commentator, 'is fraught with pitfalls for both hosts and guests.'

The important thing is to know the rules. Usually, weekends begin on Friday evening and end after Sunday lunch. The hostess may invite you to stay to tea but my advice would be to leave in the early afternoon. If it's a grand house, your bag will be unpacked for you. It's well to remember this if you are in the habit of taking a bottle of gin wrapped in your knickers for late night top-ups.

The whole business of tipping is extremely tricky. If you don't tip when it is *de rigueur*, you are damned as a skinflint, and if you offer a tip when you shouldn't, you are made to feel vulgar. After I had interviewed movie star Katharine Hepburn at her house in New York, she asked me if I knew the city. I said not terribly well. So with great kindness and charm she said that her German chauffeur would take me on a tour of districts I would never normally see on my own. I went with him to collect the car from the nearby garage. He took me through Harlem and Greenwich Village and, as he drove, he gave a fascinating running commentary on each area, its people and its history. When he dropped me at my hotel, I thanked him profusely and tried to tip him. He was utterly appalled and unmistakably felt deeply insulted. Every time I think about it, I shudder with shame and embarrassment. In retrospect, I suspect he thought that as I was a hack I was getting above my station and treating him as a servant, which was the last thought in my mind.

If you stay in a house where there is hard-working staff, they ought to be given gratuities. The current going rate is £5 a night for the person who cleans your room, and £10 a night for the cook. Social experts say that it's perfectly acceptable for hostesses to remind their guests to tip the staff but I think it should be left to the discretion of the tippers. Nevertheless, hostesses should definitely tip the staff if they employ party planners. A very famous party planner arranged a lavish wedding in the country but the bride's parents failed to tip the waiters, so when he put in his bill, he added a fictitious item for sixty-nine broken champagne glasses. The couple paid up without so much as a query and the money was then distributed between the diligent staff.

If you are invited for the weekend you need to remember that you are there for a purpose. Ned Sherrin is famed as a raconteur and wit which is why he is such a popular guest. Most country house weekends begin with a dinner party on Friday evening, which will include local guests because your hostess will want to show you off. Decide what role she has designated for you, be it joker or sophisticate, and play it to the hilt. Guests, after all, are duty-bound to sing for their supper. If you are London-based you will be expected to come up with some exciting gossip, preferably about political or sex scandals in high places. Guests can get away with behaving badly but never with being dull. A friend of mine simply invents gossip about famous actors and leading politicians which is then accepted as gospel. But no guest, however entertaining, should hog the limelight for the whole evening because everyone else will get fed up. On Saturday evening during a country house weekend, you will probably be expected to play bridge or charades. If it's the latter, all you can do is throw yourself wholeheartedly into the proceedings. The upper classes are particularly social as they have been brought up surrounded by nannies, gardeners and housekeepers and therefore don't feel any desperate need for privacy or solitude.

One always goes down to the country rather than up, irrespective of the geographical area. Things like this can be traumatic for anyone who is trying to seem posher than they really are because there is no logic behind anything. 'If you're *nouveau*,' said one posh landowner, 'and are worried about how to behave, then just ask. If you have never hunted before, it's no use trying to pretend you have or know the form.'

If you are driving, your hostess may well ask you to give a lift to other guests. My advice would be to explain that you are desolate but sadly you can't. Unfortunately, you have to make a long detour to see your elderly mother, granny or old headmaster *en route*. At the end of an exhausting weekend, you will just want to zoom off on your own. You will not want to be lumbered with a fellow guest for the entire return journey. Your hosts will lay on a plethora of entertainment and posh weekend parties often revolve around a specific event. Shooting parties start during the second week of August. The effective grouse season begins on 12 August and lasts to the end of October. Shooting has its own language and a gun means not just the firearm but the man holding it. Nowhere are class distinctions more clearly demonstrated than on a shoot. The guns are the élite and the beaters who drive the game ahead of the guns are the servants. In the old days, the shooting lunch was usually held in the open air on the moors. These days, it's often prepared by a posh girl who went to finishing school in Switzerland and is running her own business before finding a rich husband. Customarily, beaters, like officers and other ranks, eat separately. The late self-made billionaire Charlie Clore, who grew up in London's East End, was invited to a shoot at Blenheim. Everything went smoothly until he sent a message to the 10th Duke of Marlborough asking if his loader, a retired army major who taught him to shoot, could eat with the guns rather than the beaters. 'Teaching Clore to eat as well is he?' sneered Bert Marlborough.

Some women shoot but it's very rare. Occasionally, devoted girlfriends follow the shoot but on the whole it's a masculine sport. If you are invited to a country house weekend and don't want to make any mistakes, you can always obtain help and advice. 'When eating it is bad manners to hoover up your food,' Debrett instructs bossily. 'Take a little at a time and place your knife and fork across each other like swords to indicate you have not finished. During the rest of dinner you should be conversing with other guests. The form is to take your cue from your hostess. As a rule, this means women devoting the first course to the person on their left, the second to whoever is sitting on their right and then to play it by ear. It is bad manners to monopolize one person, no matter how fascinating, and to ignore another because they are boring.' This advice would have been ideal for Ted Heath, who frequently sat in total silence during dinner. One of his few women friends was so incensed by his taciturnity that she sent a note down the table with the instruction, 'Say something.' He sent her a note back saying, 'I have.' The tradition of turning to the guest on your other side after the first course has to be done with more panache and charm than was once demonstrated by Lord George Brown when he was Foreign Secretary. At a formal dinner, he was sitting next to the very attractive Edwina d'Erlanger, widow of the banker Leo d'Erlanger. He got extremely drunk and, having talked to her during the soup, suddenly said, 'I've talked to you, you old hag, long enough. I'm now going to the woman on the other side who is younger and prettier.' My theory, having met Lord George Brown and detested him, is that he was desperately socially insecure. But, because he was also clever and arrogant, he was consistently offensive to the rich and famous simply to prove to himself that he wasn't impressed by them.

Rules are not infallible. When Nancy Mitford told us all about U and non-U, we assumed she was right but Evelyn Waugh wrote to his great confidante, Ann Fleming, 'I thought Nancy's article, of which she is as proud as a peahen, great nonsense. Nancy never lived in a stately home. Swinbrook was a little house her father built and there were only women servants in it.'

Paul Burrell began as a household footman at Buckingham Palace when he was eighteen and says that the three main requirements for a good butler are 'honesty, trust and loyalty'. Recently, he wrote a book about style but anyone sticking to it rigidly could make a few mistakes. He suggests that a scented candle is a suitable offering for your hostess, which would not be wise if you want to be smart. Depending on your budget, I would suggest two glossy magazines (less than the cost of a scented candle), champagne, smoked salmon, the latest 'Harry Potter' or a whole Stilton. Do not take flowers because these have to be arranged which is the last thing a hostess wants to do as you arrive. You could always fall back on chocolates but never Black Magic or After Eights. Under no circumstances take a poinsettia which is the plant equivalent of a bottle of Blue Nun. Paul Burrell also describes pudding as 'the sweet', which is very naff. John Betjeman lampooned an imaginary lower-middle-class hostess in 'How to Get On in Society' with the verse:

Now here is a fork for your pastries
And do use the couch for your feet;
I know that I wanted to ask you –
Is trifle sufficient for sweet?

Thank-you letters should be written on the day you say farewell to your hostess. It's just as much trouble to write them a week later but they give far less pleasure. If you've been to a party, according to the widow of Lord Melchett, now Sonia Sinclair, it's best to ring up the following morning. Hostesses want instant praise which, irrespective of the truth, should be fulsome, over the top and ecstatic.

The Hon. Camilla Cecil is the social editor of *Harpers & Queen* and says, 'The best parties are planned with military precision and go off without a hitch. The ones where you can't see the joins are the ones that most thought has gone into. If people throw a party together and hope it works, most of the time it won't.' She also says that she is forever being telephoned by readers who are terrified of doing anything non-U. She invariably knows the answer to any question and can even tell them how much space one should allow for each guest at a drinks party. The answer is 4–6 square feet. She also says that no party food should be served on a cocktail stick because what do you do with the stick? The answer in my case would be to put it into my pocket. One successful businessman from a working-class background said he was traumatized when he went to a reception at Buckingham Palace and flunkeys brought round a silver platter of sausages with cocktail sticks on the side. Everyone was wondering how to get rid of the stick when they had eaten the sausage. 'No problem,' said Prince Philip, 'don't use the bloody stick.'

It's still considered rude to refuse food you are offered, although it is awkward if you are served with something which you detest. Whenever writer Leslie Thomas goes out to dinner, he gets his wife Diana to let the hostess know in advance what he doesn't like. On the whole, top toffs are prepared to eat anything but the working class is notoriously squeamish. My husband's theory is that a good public school, like prison, gets you used to dreadful meals.

Rules alter all the time, and although it used to be considered vulgar to discuss food, this has changed. You will no longer be damned as a peasant if you say something on the lines of 'This is delicious' or 'I would love to have this recipe to give to my cook.' You will be damned if you say, 'Oh, I do like bubbly' or 'Cheers' when offered a glass of champagne. My advice is always to err on the side of formality but even this can inspire mockery. When Sir Robin Day was invited to a dinner party by Woodrow Wyatt, he was introduced to the Duchess of Marlborough and addressed her as 'Your Grace'. Woodrow Wyatt wrote snootily later, 'I was very amused at his using that form of address, like a butler. With all his braggadocio Robin is unsure of himself.'

On one occasion, when writing to the Duke of Westminster, I ignored my own philosophy. I asked the *Daily Mail*'s urbane and suave diarist Nigel Dempster how I should address the Duke in a letter. 'Oh just write "Dear Duke",' he said. I followed this advice and it is absolutely correct.

Unfortunately, my lack of formality deeply offended the Duke's secretary who replied on his behalf. She was so anxious to make it clear she thought I should have called him 'Your Grace' that she put the phrase 'His Grace' in every sentence.

If you make a huge *faux pas* socially, sometimes humour can deflate the situation. One dinner-party guest mentioned that all students at a nearby university were either footballers or whores. Another guest said that actually his wife was a student at the said university. The raconteur didn't even blink but merely looked interested and said, 'Oh really, what position does she play?'

Aristocratic dinner parties are not necessarily delicious as most aristocrats have been brought up on nursery food followed by school dinners, which does little for one's palate. Their appetites have never been cosseted by a doting mummy since she was always out doing good works and bossing the villagers. This is why, on the whole, they love nanny most. 'My wife is on the bossy side,' says Andrew Cavendish, the 11th Duke of Devonshire, 'but I've always liked that in a woman.'

The worst lunch I've ever had was at the house of Lord and Lady Whitelaw. It consisted of vegetables cooked to mush and the most ghastly fatty stew. I've had better school dinners but they both ate everything with relish. The finest food I have ever had was at a dinner party given by the wife of an RAF flight lieutenant. He'd been a warrant officer who had been promoted to officer rank. All the other wives were slightly superior but ended up being full of admiration when even the chocolates were homemade and delicious. Years later, their son became hugely powerful and a billionaire in America.

Food can be tricky so, if you aren't sure, watch to see what everyone else does. Clarissa Dickson Wright says that 'Asparagus should always be eaten with fingers. It is the great class giveaway if you use a knife and fork. Mark you, I eat everything I can with my fingers. So where does that put me on the social strata?' Presumably alongside Lord Longford, who even eats his roast potatoes with his fingers, and his daughter, Lady Antonia Fraser, who has been seen in restaurants drinking soup from the bowl – yet another example of nobs getting away with behaviour that would be condemned in plebs.

Evidently, if you are offered hollandaise sauce, it should be put in a neat little dollop at the side of your plate. You can then dip each piece of asparagus into it before you eat. A friend of mine poured the sauce all over the asparagus so each time she picked up a spear she dripped sauce all down her front.

Nouveaux might be vulgar and brash but they give gloriously extravagant parties. They hire butlers to pour out the Krug in frightful glasses which look like pudding bowls on stems. They are so anxious to show off that they emulate the very vulgar Lord Archer and say, 'Have a glass of Krug.' What they mean is, 'You won't get quality stuff like this anywhere else.' *Nouveau* parties are generous even though the host does sometimes call the hired butler 'squire', shout 'Over 'ere chief,' or goose the waitresses. Often, the servants are more couth than the host as, these days, even royal servants do a bit of moonlighting. The food is sumptuous with vast sides of beef provided by party planners whom the *nouveaux* insist on calling 'the caterers'. The taste of *nouveaux* rarely improves because they are utterly confident and prone to saying, 'I know what I like,' which is lush, ornate and everything Sir Terence Conran despises.

The upper middle classes are particularly fond of giving dinner parties. If they are asked to dinner, they feel they must issue return invitations. The upper classes on the other hand are much more ruthless and rarely feel the necessity to do anything they don't want to do. They pride themselves on their breeding but sometimes behave like spoilt brats. 'I always try to invite a beautiful woman,' says one hostess. 'If she's gorgeous the men will forgive her anything. Even if she's stupid it doesn't matter. And the women love it because they can be bitchy. The competition makes them more eager to be amusing and to sparkle so they try harder.' She still follows the convention of taking the ladies off after dinner and says, 'It's so much easier for the females to do a mass exodus to powder their noses and the men, regardless of what they might say, really adore talking to each other.' I'm sure she's right and a male guest would much rather be seated next to a successful chap than the man's middle-aged, porky wife. Margaret Thatcher always refused to leave the men and stayed behind with them which made the other wives incredibly cross. Since she had so much power the men were delighted and vied for her attention. The good-looking ones who flirted with her were always her favourites. Unfortunately, Michael Heseltine's wife told me that he found it impossible to chat up Lady Thatcher, which didn't help his career.

There is something extremely unsavoury about one upper-class habit. At grand dinner parties in the country, the female guests still leave the table first. The men pass the port and then go outside, stand in a circle on the lawn and have a communal pee before joining the ladies in the drawing room. If men on a housing estate in Bolton did this, they would be in danger of getting arrested. Recently, I went to a posh dinner party in Dorset where it was the custom. Despite this, the host and hostess were right-wing sticklers for what they saw as proper behaviour. When upper-class men use the lavatory, according to Lady Celestria Noel, daughter of the Earl of Gainsborough, 'They tend to leave the door open. It's almost always not locked which is a legacy I imagine of prep and public school days when cubicles had no doors.' It's also a legacy of a class which doesn't care about the effect their behaviour has on anyone else. It doesn't concern them that they might embarrass or upset people, which is both the strength and the Achilles heel of the upper classes.

The upper middles collect endless recipes from the posh Sunday papers and are very influenced by what they read. Many of the wives went on cookery courses before they got married and are dab hands at doing clever things with filo pastry. The emphasis is on healthy eating and the marathon, cream-laden dinner parties of my early married life are long gone. If the host and hostess share the cooking, they will probably have a thundering big row before the guests arrive. Older hosts still offer spirits but younger ones now tend to serve champagne with the pre-prandials. Years ago, I interviewed the late Lord Sieff of Marks & Spencer and he said, 'The champagne in our stores is good enough to offer to one's guests. I'm not so sure about the wine.' Their wine list has improved since then but their cheapest champagne is still drinkable. Some hostesses ask the gentlemen to change seats after every course but I think it's a terrible idea and just unsettles everyone. I am sure Raine Spencer does this as she runs her dinner parties with the discipline of a general. 'I'm like Mummy,' she said to me, 'very *détailliste*.' Also, she has natural authority, so that when she wants people to move, they move. She even dictates the seating plan when she takes people to the cinema or the theatre and watching Raine marshalling her guests is a diverting sight.

There was a time when children were in bed long before guests arrived and the upper classes still want children to be banished well before dinner. But in middle-class circles they are to be seen passing round the potato sticks and peanuts or, when the hostess is really pushing the boat out, prawn wantons from Marks & Spencer. Upper-class children have a social life all their own, and in the summer, vast numbers of them congregate in the Cornish villages of Rock and Polzeath where their mummies and daddies have holiday houses. They surf the breakers during the day, and in the evening, make bonfires on Daymer beach. They drink vodka, lemonade and lime, smoke Silk Cut Ultra Milds and dance to Sex Bomb blaring from a ghettoblaster. Locals call the area Kensington-on-Sea and the accents of the posh teenagers are more than proof that class is here to stay.

The pecking order at dinner parties still survives. This is very irritating if you are seated on your host's left, which means you are deemed to be the least important guest or the wife of the least-reckoned chap. All too often in the new century, it is still the profession of the man which places a couple in a social context. Even these days, a man is judged by his job and a woman by her looks. This may be why upper-class polo groupies won't sleep with a player with a handicap lower than five.

Prince Edward continues to say we live in an egalitarian society but he'd be none too pleased, not to say amazed, if he went to a dinner party and was placed on his hostess's left. I've never known anyone who didn't instantly register where they have been positioned at any 'function' (which is a very lower-middle-class word). If they think they have been relegated to a position below their status, they are inwardly incensed. 'Those who matter don't mind and those who mind don't matter,' said a *grande dame* who was involved in arranging seating plans according to protocol at Buckingham Palace banquets. This is not a theory which I either believe or trust. The people who matter in terms of social standing are the ones who always get top-notch treatment so, of course, they don't mind. Princess Michael has a dramatic sense of her own importance and says, 'The fact is, of those who married into the family since Prince Philip, I have more royal blood.' She also claims she had to be persuaded to get married by Lord Mountbatten because she was not 'remotely interested in Prince Michael'. This may well be true but she was certainly interested in becoming a princess.

Hardy Amies would have relished the grand party thrown by Princess Michael for her son Lord Frederick Windsor's twenty-first and her daughter Lady Gabriella's nineteenth birthdays. Sent out with the invitations was a lyrical explanation of the theme of the party: '. . . Traditionally, the King of France invited guests to partake of a *dîner champêtre* . . . a royal celebration of summer and roses. As for costumes – courtiers and their ladies promenading, swashbuckling highwaymen and hussars, milkmaids and yokels.' Five hundred guests dressed as members of the eighteenth-century French court and dined on spit-roasted hogs, washed down with champagne. Princess Michael has made it quite clear that she is indifferent to the opinions of *hoi polloi*. 'I'm not going to have sleepless nights,' she says contemptuously, 'worrying about what the good citizens of Newcastle are thinking about me.'

It's quite useful to have a dramatic opening line when you go to a party. One of the best I have ever heard was a chap who introduced himself to me by saying, 'I'm Augustus John's last bastard.' Then I met a man who said, 'Oh we're new to the village. The family only moved here in 1640. We got the house in Cromwell's time. He confiscated it so we bought it cheap.' The only boastful thing I could come up with in return was to point to my ring and say, 'This is the ring the Czar of Russia gave to my husband's Great Uncle Pat who was his surgeon.' Prince Charles has quite an original line in chat and tells his guests that his good friend the Duke of Westminster 'employs more butlers than I do'.

Unfortunately, few of us can compete with the 11th Duke of Atholl. He's the only man in Europe with the right to his own private army, the Atholl Highlanders. Apparently, in 1845 Queen Victoria went to stay at Blair Castle and the 6th Duke provided a posse of Highlanders to look after her. The Queen was so impressed she awarded the Duke the right to bear arms.

Recently, I was having dinner with my daughter in Clarke's restaurant in London's Kensington Church Street which is widely patronized by the rich and famous. Our second course was guinea fowl served with vegetables artistically arranged in a muslin bag which was tied up with string. Initially, I wasn't quite sure what it was. I thought of the days when I would have been so fazed by the muslin parcel that I wouldn't have realized I was expected to untie the string and take out the vegetables. I may well have tried to cut up the bag and eat the entire thing. If you don't know how to eat something, there is absolutely nothing wrong in asking for help. Unfortunately, when you really need help is usually the time when you don't have the confidence to ask for it. Today, if I did something so silly, I'd be amused, but it's been a long, tricky road to get to the position where I wouldn't be absolutely mortified.

I had lunch with some hugely rich friends and the host knocked his red wine over the damask tablecloth. He laughed, called for another bottle and said, 'Put the tablecloth on my bill.' There was much merriment and we were all entertained, but if he hadn't been suave and rich, it would have been cringe-making. He would have felt humiliated and we'd have thought he was clumsy and gauche. I am afraid that such incidents are judged in different ways depending on who is involved. If a billionaire aristocrat ordered crème de menthe *frappé*, I would find it rather endearing. If my father had ordered it, there was a time when I'd have been embarrassed. I know that is pathetic and utterly stupid but it's the truth, even though it's shaming. I once went to lunch at Downing Street when Margaret Thatcher was Prime Minister. Pre-lunch drinks were brought round on a tray which had a specimen drink of every variety including a gin and tonic, a whisky and soda and a glass of sherry. After lunch, Lady Thatcher had crème de menthe *frappé* with her coffee and said, 'Denis thinks it's terribly vulgar.' Years later, I went to a dinner party at Chequers after Tony Blair became Prime Minister and the pre-prandial drinks were champagne. But then, Mr Blair, unlike Maggie, has a middle-class background.

The lower middle class are a social lot and their favourite method of entertaining is 'the barbie'. They invite all the neighbours and the main intention of the evening is to boast like mad. They invite the ladies to use what they call the 'little girls' room' so they can show off the bidet, the circular bath and the mauve-coloured, quilted lavatory paper. While the steaks are sizzling on the gas barbecue, they hand out paper plates and paper napkins which they call 'serviettes'. These are so smart and amusing they are printed with pictures of naked ladies. There are steak knives and forks with carved handles and paper umbrellas in the drinks. The host does the cooking wearing a huge chef's hat and shorts to show off the mahogany tan he got on the family holiday in Spain. The hostess hands round a large bowl of coleslaw and wears skin-tight turquoise trousers, yellow stilettos and a purple bustier. She totters around hoping people will admire her cleavage and rotating her shoulders in time to the stereo which is blaring out Tom Jones singing 'It's Not Unusual'. When people say she looks like Sheryl Gascoigne, she gives the kind of raucous laugh which could easily smash the gold-trimmed chandelier in the 'lounge' overlooking the rockery. The children are much in evidence with the little girls dressed to look like burgeoning Spice Girls with bare midriffs and cropped tops.

If the upper middles throw a barbecue it tends to be Sunday lunch and the food on offer is often fish marinated in herbs and served with salads from the *River Café Cook Book*. In the late afternoon, there are mixed doubles on the En-tout-cas tennis court while nannies take the children for rides on the family ponies.

Working-class parties are not pretentious because the working classes, like top toffs, feel no desire to impress. The emphasis is on beer which has been brought back from a day trip to Calais. In my youth, women rarely drank but this has changed so there will be Southern Comfort and lemonade or snowballs for wives, girlfriends and daughters. The days when working-class women were wonderful bakers have long gone so there will be crisps, tinned-tuna sandwiches, pork pies and meat pasties from Iceland. Then they will sing along to a karaoke machine and, later, the host and his mates will go down to the local shopping centre to bring back a Chinese takeaway.

Twenty years ago they wouldn't have dreamed of touching what they called 'foreign muck'. However, package tours on the Costa Brava have made them much more adventurous.

10

BOUNDERS, ECCENTRICS AND SHOPKEEPERS

Bounders are chameleons and experts at infiltrating the worlds they wish to inhabit. They are, indeed, a class of their own and come from all backgrounds. They are driven by a passionate determination to use other people, usually women, for their own advantage. Mostly, they are in the pursuit of money, sex, influence, aggrandizement or, in some cases, power. They are brilliant at understanding what women want and are perfectly willing to provide it. They are superb listeners and will sit for hours as a woman pours out her insecurities and fears.

One of the most charismatic bounders I've ever met was billionaire Jimmy Goldsmith, who adhered to the principle that when you marry your mistress, you create a vacancy. At the time of his death, he had been married three times and was living with his French mistress Laure Boulay de la Meurthe. When he and I met, we had lunch together in Laurent, the restaurant he owned in the centre of Paris. Afterwards we went for a walk in the park. He held my arm and I was captivated. He was mesmeric, imperious and a bit like a domineering hero in a Mills & Boon novel.

Jimmy Goldsmith had been at Eton with the sons of famous aristocratic families but he inculcated in his daughter Jemima the belief that British aristocrats are the most decadent and useless in the world. Sir James was half-Jewish, half-French and a Roman Catholic. There were times in his youth when he felt patronized and, as he had a vengeful nature, there may have been an underlying anger in his convictions. He was such a believer in 'an eye for an eye' that he planned an inspired revenge on his house master who he felt had treated him unfairly. It was the custom at Eton for boys to give their house master a present when they left. Jimmy Goldsmith's house master was a passionate lover of classical music so the young Goldsmith bought eight of the finest recordings. He handed them to his house master, and as the grateful teacher thanked him profusely, the boy picked them up one by one and smashed them.

Throughout Jimmy Goldsmith's life, upper-class girls fell in love with him but mostly he broke their hearts. This didn't deflect them and they pursued him even more shamelessly because top-drawer girls are frequently over-sexed, pre-datory and terrifyingly uninhibited.

Bounders are adept at making a girl feel unique and special and they possess foolproof chat-up lines. Unlike other men, bounders are more than happy to adopt the mores, manners, phrases and idiosyncrasies of the rich and influential. Middle-class bounders can become mesmerized more with the lifestyle than with the girl. James Hewitt fell in love with a princess who was above his station. Ultimately, he turned his affair with Diana, Princess of Wales, into an income for life. Now he dresses in bespoke suits, drives an expensive car and lives in a £300,000 Chelsea flat. He looks like the gentleman he always yearned to be but never was and never will be. The Princess was not a snob and falling in love with a chap who was her social inferior would not have worried her. After her marriage broke up, Diana became terribly lonely and often went from Kensington Palace to her butler Paul Burrell's house to chat to his wife Maria. Even as a child she would spend hours in the kitchen and had a natural rapport with people from all classes. She stayed with James Hewitt at his mother's cottage and loved to tidy the cupboards.

After Diana's death, Mr Hewitt had a succession of girlfriends but then had a liaison with wealthy divorcee Kate Simon who was ten years his senior. She was said to be deeply in love with him and I suspect the situation had something in common with a scene in John Braine's novel *Room at the Top*. When the ambitious social climber Joe Lampton seduces the heiress daughter of an affluent northern businessman, she asks him how much he loves her. 'A hundred thousand pounds' worth, love,' he says. 'A hundred thousand pounds' worth.'

Bounders perfect their script early on in their seducing career and rarely deviate. Why should they when it has proved so effective? Sir George Martin's actor son Greg used all his tried-and-tested ploys to woo Tara Palmer Tomkinson and she fell for them and him hook, line and sinker. He told her that no one would ever love her as he loved her, that he wanted her to have his babies and they would live in the country in a romantic house with an Aga and have a Labrador. She was bewitched until she discovered that he'd spun other women exactly the same tale. He's made a career out of smooth seduction and is a better actor in real life than he is in movies. He met Tara at Mick Jagger's birthday party and turned his powerful, experienced charm on her with the intensity of a spotlight. He trotted out his well-rehearsed spiel and she was hooked. 'He was very handsome,' she says, 'and he had such charisma.'

He told me I was the only one for him and that I was the most beautiful girl in the room. He made me feel a million dollars. He knew everything about me. He made me feel safe and I had felt so unsafe for such a long time. He got a clairvoyant to come round and do my horoscope. And he wanted me to meet his son. He said, 'You'll get on so well, he'll love you.' He was so excited, he was like a little child himself. But he was just completely full of lies. He said, 'What you really need is a strong man,' which was music to my ears. He can convince you of anything.

If ever a girl meets a man who never gets cross, has unlimited patience, doesn't want to talk about himself, is passionately interested in the minutiae of her life, plucks his eyebrows, tells her he wants to walk barefoot with her in the sand and rings at dawn to say, 'The rising sun is almost as beautiful as you,' she's probably met a bounder. James Hewitt skilfully managed to persuade Princess Diana, when she was still married to Prince Charles, that somehow one day they could get married, have children and live normal, cosy, ordinary lives. Bounders are marvellous at conjuring up a magical fantasy world and making it sound feasible. They also know that women have an extraordinary capacity to swallow the most outrageous flattery. 'You can't lay it on too thick,' one cad told me and I am afraid he's right. A bounder can convince a plain woman that she is a goddess, a fatty that she is Venus de Milo and a boring one that she is an enchantress. He can even assure a middle-aged heiress that he loves her for the vulnerable, insecure inner little girl which only he can see.

Bounders never say tedious things like 'You look OK to me.' Unlike most men, they are prepared to provide endless reassurance and praise. They are never distracted or too tired for sex. They are thrillingly poetic, over the top, lavish with compliments and make wildly romantic, generous gestures. Unfortunately, these gestures are most likely to be funded by the woman. Middle- and working-class bounders are rarely attracted to paupers. They have an unerring instinct for vulnerability and wealth and know precisely the chat-up line which will work.

There are, of course, upper-class bounders although they are usually after sex and not social enhancement. They rarely marry out of their class but are quite prepared to fornicate with the lower classes. Colin Clark is the son of art historian Lord Clark, and as a young man he used his posh connections to get a job as gofer on the set of the movie *The Prince and the Showgirl* which starred Sir Laurence Olivier and Marilyn Monroe.

He has published two memoirs of those days and, in the first, writes of his lustful pursuit of a lower-middle-class girl he patronizingly calls 'little wardrobe girl' or 'Wdg' for short. He pursues her, charms her and woos her. 'The little Wdg,' he wrote, 'is as sweet and tasty as a sugar mouse. I can't resist her.' Later, he dumped her and broke her heart. She was all right for a convenient fling but not to be introduced into his own social world. On one occasion, he did take her back to the servants' quarters of his parents' Albany flat when they weren't there but that was as far as she got. He was invited to a party given by the playwright Sir Terence Rattigan and had to explain to the little wardrobe girl that he couldn't possibly take her along. After the end of their affair, when clearly her lower-middle-class ambitions had bored him, he wrote, 'Alas there is nothing I can do. It is over. Poor little Wdg. She'll probably be married in a couple of years. Two kids and a family car, Wdg heaven.' Colin Clark sounds snobbish and pretty unpleasant. The poor little wardrobe girl never stood a chance, as her vowels and gentility began to jar on his upper-class nerves.

The late Alan Clark was his glitteringly handsome older brother, known in his youth by mothers of débutantes as 'NSIT'– short for 'Not Safe In Taxis'. Over many philandering years, he proved that if you are clever and witty you can get away with being a bounder. He was consistently unfaithful but adored his wife Jane. 'Flirting for Al is a sort of ritual,' she said, 'but I can keep him under control. I know how much rein I can give him. I can pull him back as though he were on one of those dog leads.' She was more than capable of coping with her husband, and when he went too far, she threw things at him including, on one occasion, an axe.

Jonathan Aitken definitely has bounderlike qualities. He had an affair with Lady Thatcher's daughter Carol but probably, at the time, he was pursuing power by association rather than money. He's an old Etonian who lost everything after he was sent to Belmarsh Prison for perjury. When he got there, he thought how irrelevant the class system was. 'Who cares about accents and upbringings?' he said. 'These are external things, what really matters are human hearts and souls and behaviour. There are some of my prison-class friends I would trust as much as my upper-class friends. I really think that as a result of prison I've gone colour blind and class blind. It just never enters my head any more.' He said this but admitted that there was a pecking order in prison. The ground rules might have changed but the natural human instinct to put people into categories still remains. Evidently, the top toffs in prison are what are known as the Big Faces. 'They're the chaps who've been on "Wanted" posters,' explained Jonathan. 'They're the blaggers or tool-men which means big armed robbers. People say, "Oh he's only a wheel man, I'm a toolman," meaning, "On raids he only drove the car. I carried the gun.'" There is an accepted hierarchical system even behind bars and the strongest people rise to the top.

The upper classes can be extremely offensive. They assume their every impulse must be instantly fulfilled and are completely oblivious to the fact that their servants either need or want a private life. Aristocrats have always been drawn to the *beau monde* and, these days, beautiful models have replaced the variety stars who in the last century were so adored by top toffs. Bea Lillie became Lady Peel and Gertrude Lawrence, who caught the eye of the Duke of Kent, nearly married the upper-class Philip Astley. He was born at Chequers, the Buckinghamshire mansion now used as a weekend retreat by successive prime ministers. 'Philip,' said Gertie, 'was christened in the robes of Oliver Cromwell and educated at Eton and the Royal Military College.' She was ashamed of her own working-class background in Clapham and her continuing love affairs with a series of aristocrats helped her to rewrite her past. These days, stunning models such as Jerry Hall and Liz Hurley are part of the aristocratic world, having been blessed with looks, wit and total confidence. Beautiful women and aristocrats elicit admiration, compliance and anxiety to please in those around them, which is why both groups have such self-belief, poise and *élan*. Ms Hurley's great friend is Henry Dent Brocklehurst, and Jerry is close to Teddy St Aubyn. He's a cousin of Lord St Levan and part of an old landed Cornish family whose pedigree stretches back to the Norman Conquest. Jerry Hall comes from a poor background in Texas and is the daughter of a violent father. She left home at sixteen to live in the YWCA in Paris. She found work as a model and never looked back. 'Long legs help,' she says. Now, wherever she goes, there is a waiting minion and a chauffeur-driven limousine and underneath her dazzling charm is the unconscious hauteur of the seriously rich. She stayed with Mick Jagger for twenty-two years so clearly is drawn to bounders. After they divorced, she played alluring seductress Mrs Robinson in the stage version of *The Graduate* and said before the show opened, 'You need a certain amount of ego to play the seductress, to get up on stage and take your clothes off in front of everybody. Ego only gets dangerous when you put yourself above someone else.'

When playwright Alfred Shaughnessy was a very young man, like most aristocrats of his era, he was an *habitué* at deb dances which were strictly chaperoned. After dancing with demure virgins of his own class, he and his friends went to sleazy night clubs where pretty working-class girls worked as dance hostesses. 'You'd pick one out and say, "I'd like her to join me,"' he told me. 'You then had to buy a bottle of champagne for the privilege of sitting with her. It was all very respectable on the surface. There was no overt commitment to sex and you'd say, "Would you like to come and dance?" You'd have a little foxtrot, she'd be very beautifully dressed but when she opened her mouth and started to talk she'd have a cockney accent. The hostesses weren't allowed to leave till the club closed which meant yawning your way through until 3 a.m. Then you could take her home in a taxi to some seedy little flat in Kilburn. Some would pour out their troubles to you. I got fond of one or two but it was mainly the sex drive. There was another place called the Bag of Nails which was an out-and-out brothel in Kingly Street. A lot of the young nobs would go straight there after deb dances.'

The debs, with the exception of the occasional fast flirt,

were virginal and innocent. Unmarried pregnancies were almost unheard-of and twenty-five-year-old brides knew nothing about sex. The third Viscountess Astor married Bill Astor when she was the Hon. Sarah Norton. In due course, he inherited the Astor title, a vast fortune and Cliveden. This is the wonderful house on the Thames near Maidenhead where in 1961 Christine Keeler met the then Minister for War, John Profumo. Their affair caused the scandal that led to the downfall of the Macmillan government. The Astors divorced but Sarah, now Mrs Baring, says, 'I was totally ignorant. Certainly I and all my close friends would have considered ourselves defiled if we hadn't come to marriage as virgins. Even after you had become engaged it made no difference. Virginity lasted until the wedding night. The boys weren't innocent but that wasn't expected of them.' The upper-class girls with their posh voices were seen as untouchable. The working-class tarts with their cockney accents were sexy enough to sleep with but not suitable to be introduced to a chap's mummy.

Bounders are self-aware, self-conscious, predatory and never do anything without thinking it through. They are always acting and giving a performance. Eccentrics, on the other hand, form a group which encompasses people from all social backgrounds but they do share certain characteristics. They are, on the whole, so bound up in their own passions that they are distinctly uninhibited. Eccentrics are never judgemental. The driving force behind most eccentrics, be they inventors, actors or painters, is their work which is their life. Rarely do they have the time or inclination for things which concern the rest of us, like convention or social niceties.

Lucinda Lambton, daughter of Lord Lambton, is an upper-class eccentric so the combination makes her terrifyingly unselfconscious. She's hugely talented as an artist and writer but almost childlike in her spontaneous behaviour. There is neither pretence, nor veneer. She says exactly what she thinks and appears to have no fear of anything or anyone. I interviewed her and her future husband, Sir Peregrine Worsthorne, over lunch at the Ritz and she dipped her fork greedily into his food and forcibly told him off when she disagreed with him. I was asking them about their passionate affair in middle age and Lucinda suddenly decided that they really ought not to talk about their love for publication. 'Romance is undoubtedly of interest,' she said, 'but I still don't think it warrants the vanity of talking about it. How can you,' she asked her fiancé, 'a man of sage wisdom and distinction, do this?' Peregrine Worsthorne replied gently, 'What you're saying is people like you don't talk to the general public.' This was like a red rag to a bull and Lucy exploded, 'I'm not saying that at all. That's a real snooty, horrible thing to say. People like us, I've never said such a thing in my life. Only a snooty mind would think up such a snooty sentiment. It's an appalling, atrocious thing to say.' The dialogue might have come straight out of *Private Lives* but they were both unaware of their surroundings, me or the other guests in the restaurant who were gripped and greatly entertained.

Cookery writer Josceline Dimbleby is the daughter of a gentle, upper-class, wealthy eccentric who had a passion for jazz and fireworks. Her father would spend two years designing more and more dramatic fireworks. Then he'd throw a spectacular firework party, two years' work would go up in smoke and he would begin again. When their father died, Josceline's half-brother Ben arranged a fantastic bouquet of fireworks which was placed on top of the coffin.

He asked the organist at the funeral to play jazz and the priest came down the aisle as the organist was belting out 'Nobody's Sweetheart'. Afterwards, Ben placed the bouquet of fireworks on his father's lawn and set it alight.

'Eccentrics,' says Dr David Weeks, author of *Eccentrics: The Scientific Investigation*, 'have an overriding curiosity that drives them on and makes them oblivious to the irritations and stresses of daily life that plague the rest of us. They don't try to keep up with the Joneses, they don't worry about conforming and they usually have a firm belief that they are right and the rest of the world is wrong.'

I have a theory that people who are born into grand society feel the same way because they never have to adapt, learn or pretend. When filmmaker Duncan Roy impersonated Lord Rendlesham for a joke, he said, 'If people think you have a title you are immediately empowered. The sons and daughters of rich people have a kind of history and people have a point of interest and connection with you. When I said I was Lord Rendlesham I didn't have to be me.' In other words, when you have a title, people are automatically interested in you which gives you confidence. You can be boring and tedious, but if you have a stately home, people put up with you. 'He's an old bore, not very bright and the house is icy,' Noël Coward wrote about the Duke of Marlborough. If the Duke had been plain Mr Bert Marlborough living in a chilly council house in Wigan, he would have been avoided like the plague. But he lived at Blenheim Palace so glamorous, captivating, famous guests were always delighted to be invited to amuse their host. This is the main reason behind the continuing liaisons between aristocrats and the showbusiness élite. Stephen Fry and Emma Thompson are frequently asked to Highgrove where they entertain Prince Charles. It never, of course, crosses HRH's mind that he himself might be boring, heavy-going or lachrymose. He is the Prince of Wales and that is enough.

'Is it rude?' asked the Prince before the première of a new movie. The Prince, who has at times behaved like a bounder, frequently sounds as though he's still an awkward seven-year-old who thinks words like 'tits' and 'bum' are the wittiest he's ever heard – scarcely surprising in a man who talks about Tampax during late-night, romantic chats. He and his brothers share a lavatorial sense of humour. This, I imagine, is due to being brought up by authoritarian nannies who were obsessive about potty training.

The Duke of Westminster knew when he was sixteen that one day he would be the richest man in Britain and own a massive chunk of London. He also has 13,000 acres in Cheshire where he lives at Eaton Hall. He met his wife Natalia at a party given by the Duke of Marlborough at Blenheim Palace. The Duchess is the granddaughter of the late Lady Zia Wernher who was the daughter of the Grand Duke Michael of Russia. These days in Cheshire, the Westminsters are local royalty. When Gyles Brandreth was MP for Chester, the Duke and Duchess allowed the City of Chester Conservative Association Annual Salmon Supper to be held at Eaton Hall or as Mr Brandreth wrote acidly in his diary at the time, 'The event isn't so much at Eaton Hall itself as in the garage at Eaton Hall. We huddle together for warmth as we dine *al fresco* in a cobbled yard bordered by garages and stables. We are very grateful to be adjacent to such grand surroundings despite the wind and the rains. I sit next to Her Grace and my banter comes across as over-familiarity and, as she glazes over, I can't think what more to say.' Naturally, duchesses never worry about what to say as they know that people are impressed by their mere presence.

Scratch the genealogy of a top toff and it's amazing how many working-class skeletons emerge. I'd always assumed that Nancy Mitford must be the epitome of upper-class confidence. However, the late arch snob Anthony Powell wrote in his journals, 'Nancy could be funny in conversation but never at all at ease, always desperately self-conscious, a condition that continued through her life. Her mother's father was illegitimate issue of a Liberal MP called Bowles and a housemaid.' Possibly, Nancy Mitford inherited her self-consciousness from her working-class great-granny. Nancy's sister is the Duchess of Devonshire who has proved to be a first-rate businesswoman. She's made a tremendous success of running her magnificent stately home Chatsworth as a business, with a garden centre, gift shop, restaurant, bar and farm shop selling Chatsworth marmalade and Chatsworth sausages.

The prices are high and the knowledge that the shopkeeper is a duchess is obviously an asset to trade. Upper-class women like playing at shop and they make persuasive saleswomen because they have authoritative voices which brook no opposition. In fact, a lot of nobs have gone into trade and have an unfair advantage over their rivals. Countess Spencer was terrifically successful at persuading visitors to buy over-priced goods when she and her husband opened a shop on the Althorp estate. She was even prepared to sell her signature on postcards or bottles of wine. 'My father would have been appalled to see me serving in a shop,' said Lord Spencer, 'but I enjoy it.' Raine Spencer was so organized that when I interviewed her she arrived with an alarm clock to ensure we stopped at the precise designated time. She's utterly merciless, uses charm as a kind of battering ram and is never off guard.

Prince Charles is the most famous shopkeeper in the world with his souvenir establishment at Highgrove. It's open only to invited groups such as gardening organizations. 'You must visit my shop,' he says. One of the most popular items is a £20 silver-plated letter opener which is irrefutably naff. One of the reasons the business is so successful is because the shop is run by a team of forty-six unpaid local volunteers. It's a smart marketing ploy by HRH. He gets free labour but the women providing it feel privileged to get the chance which sounds remarkably like exploitation.

Viscount Linley is another royal shopkeeper. He sells hand-carved furniture in his Chelsea shop which opened in 1985 and owes a lot of its success to his name. If he wasn't twelfth in line to the throne, few people would know the shop existed. Certainly, he is unlikely to have had so many commissions from millionaires like Elton John. 'Being a member of the royal family is a disadvantage for a shopkeeper,' he says absurdly, 'because it means people are scared to come in the door.' I think he underrates the courage of the public since it's the high prices that keep us out. Like Prince Edward, he trades on his name but refuses to accept that it gives him unrivalled advantage over unknown carpenters. He ought to be grateful for his invaluable press coverage and the powerful, wealthy clients he gets. This is due in no small part to snobbery and the fact that the Queen is his aunty. 'All men fall into two main divisions,' said writer Norman Douglas, 'those who value human relationships and those who value social or financial advancements. The first division are gentlemen. The second division are cads.'

ARE YOU TOO ANXIOUS TO PLEASE?

	Yes	No
1 If someone bumps into you, are you the one who apologizes?	☐	☐
2 Do you assume the accent of the person you are talking to?	☐	☐
3 Would you prefer to see a film which is the preference of your companion rather than your own?	☐	☐
4 Do you wait to see what other members of your party choose to eat in a restaurant before you decide?	☐	☐
5 Do you laugh even when you don't understand the joke?	☐	☐
6 Would you accept the worst table in a restaurant?	☐	☐
7 Do you invariably agree with the opinions of your poshest acquaintance?	☐	☐
8 Do you find it impossible to complain?	☐	☐
9 Do you leave a tip even when the service is terrible?	☐	☐

10 Would you politely eat shrimps at a dinner
    party even if you knew you'd break
    out in a rash later?   ☐ ☐

If you answered 'yes' to 4 or more of these questions, it's
    time to get more assertive.
If you answered 'yes' to between 1 and 3 of these questions,
    you're just a very nice person.

11

MARRYING UP

'Marriage is so much easier with a woman from one's own class,' Lord Lichfield said and he is, of course, absolutely right. My advice to anyone thinking of marrying somebody who comes from a different social background would be, 'Think again.' If the girl is the posh half of the couple, I'd make my warning twice as strong because women are much more adaptable than chaps. Men yearn to be in control so they are offended by any suggestion that they should change their behaviour or their speech. If they are criticized about the way they hold their knife, drink soup or use the term 'front room', they are liable to turn nasty. 'Why can't the posh girl adapt instead?' you may well ask. However, being realistic I'm afraid that, usually, all the adjusting has to be done upwards.

If you have always said 'drawing room', 'lavatory', 'salt cellar' or 'vegetables', you are not going to start saying 'lounge', 'toilet', 'cruet' or 'greens'. Having married above my station, I'm the one who has changed my speech and my behaviour. Now you can take me anywhere. The only effect I've had on my husband's speech is that when he gets home he says, 'Hello, love.' Playwright Alfred Shaughnessy's wife had a similar experience. Alfred, who is always known as Freddie, wrote scripts for the hugely popular television drama series *Upstairs Downstairs*. He fictionalized his own early life of wealth and privilege and based one of the main characters, James Bellamy, on himself. He was educated at

Eton and Sandhurst and his grandfather was Lord Shaughnessy. His stepfather was the Hon. Sir Piers Legh who was Equerry to the Prince of Wales. Freddie grew up in St James's Palace surrounded by formality and royal grandeur and with a fiercely snobbish mother. He was charming and handsome and, understandably, Lady Legh assumed her eminently eligible son would marry an heiress.

Then Freddie fell passionately in love with a Yorkshire girl from Hull who was the daughter of a seaman. She was a staggeringly beautiful model and, when they first met, he was overwhelmed. 'Eventually I told my mama and she said, "Who is she?" I said, "She comes from Hull but that's immaterial because I love her dearly." Mama wanted me to marry some duke's daughter and she said, "You've got so little in common."'

Freddie couldn't be deflected and, having proposed to Jean and been accepted, he went to Yorkshire to formally ask Jean's father for her hand. In those days, upper-class girls brought a dowry to marriage, but when Freddie tentatively mentioned this, his future father-in-law was outraged. 'He's getting you,' he shouted to his daughter. 'Isn't that enough?' I rather share his feelings and find something pretty shameful in the old-fashioned, aristocratic belief that future husbands needed to be bought.

Ultimately, the Shaughnessys married in London at St James's Church and, nearly fifty years later, they laughed about Lady Legh's angry, sour face in all their wedding pictures. Jean was fiercely proud and initially thought, 'They'll have to take me as I am.' Inevitably, she changed. 'I said things like "pardon" and 'I'll have a sherry," instead of "a glass of sherry",' she told me. 'But if you want things to go smoothly you have to learn the language and in the end I did.'

When she and her husband first met, she had already lost her Yorkshire accent and this was probably crucial. If Jean had retained her Yorkshire dialect, I imagine the besotted young Freddie would have had a few reservations.

'Who cares about family background these days?' asked Marina Ogilvy, daughter of Princess Alexandra, when she ran off with a working-class photographer who was the son of a trumpet-playing bricklayer. It's an age-old bleat from those struggling to find their own identity but feeling suffocated by powerful parents. In her youth, Marina made the common mistake of believing that everything about her illustrious background was a disadvantage and everything in the ordinary life she craved must be commendable and worthwhile. Clearly, for a time she thought that every working-class family is comforting and all-embracing as opposed to her own formal, disciplined parents. She turned up her well-bred nose at privilege, money and influence. Chillingly, she condemned her father as an unpleasant, heavy-drinking, royal toady and her mother as cold-hearted and remote. 'My mother wasn't there for me when it counted,' she cried.

Marina revelled in her emotions and appeared to despise her mother whose impenetrable public face hid a lot of anguish. Princess Alexandra was brought up to believe that duty came before personal happiness and that family problems should not be aired in public. When her only daughter kicked over the traces with vulgar abandon, she never uttered one word of criticism. She didn't reveal if she was hurt, embarrassed, ashamed or devastated. She remained outwardly imperturbable as her daughter was pictured dressed from head to toe in black leather astride a motorbike and in other pictures nearly naked. She was also pictured on a throne surrounded by corgis, wearing a crown and a PVC jumpsuit.

Ten years later, Marina's love affair followed by marriage to her lower-middle-class husband had palled. Like many men who marry above their station, he was so determined to put her in her place that he lost her. 'I don't live in the shadow of wifey,' he said angrily. They were brought up with different attitudes, values and customs. They married in 1990 when Marina was five months pregnant and by 1996 there were reports of rows and violence. Finally, on their son Christian's fifth birthday, Marina left her husband and their semi-detached house in south-west London. Later that year, she was awarded an uncontested quickie divorce on the grounds of his unreasonable behaviour. *Au fond*, she is her mother's daughter and she fled to the security and privacy of her parents' large house in Richmond Park. She'd had her foray into the wide-open plebeian world and found it chilly and frightening. She's now back in the close-knit, protective, royal circle and I suspect she will never step outside it again. When all your life you have been treated as special, unique and important, it's not easy being seen as merely one of the common herd. Marina believed that if she threw off the strictures of her royal status she would find her true self, but she felt trapped by what she had mistakenly believed to be freedom. We are all the product of our upbringing and we seldom escape from that influence, be it good or bad.

When she was young, Marina thought her parents were cold and aloof. Possibly, after seven years with an emotional, noisy, volatile man, she has discovered that she actually prefers her parents' formality and restraint. She no longer believes that family background is irrelevant and meaningless. Some men are impressed by wealth and privilege but almost all those who marry socially superior wives then go on to be unfaithful or violent. Men like to be in control, so if they feel inferior to their wives they have to do something to feel in charge.

Another marriage between two people from different backgrounds was that of the Marchioness of Londonderry and musician Georgie Fame. He grew up in the same small Lancashire town as I did but gifted musicians become virtually classless. They have an arrogance and confidence which transcend class. The most important thing in their lives is talent. If you have it then that is all that matters. The destructive qualities which hold back working-class people who want to move upwards socially are lack of confidence, embarrassment or fear of making a fool of oneself.

If you marry above your station, it's invariably you who is apologizing for your family. This is despite the fact that your husband or wife may have ghastly parents or siblings. People who marry somebody from a different class have major problems if one of them isn't prepared to change. When political commentator Brian Walden met upper-class girl Jane McKerron, it was a *coup de foudre*. They married but it was a stormy relationship and there were difficulties over the dramatic contrast in their upbringings. Her father was Sir Patrick McKerron, acting Governor of Singapore after the war, and Jane spent her childhood in the grandeur of Government House. Brian Walden grew up in West Bromwich where his father was an unemployed glazier. 'I come from an upper-class colonial background,' said Jane, 'and Brian comes from the slums, as he would say himself. I had a very grand life as a small child. I had my own groom, my own chauffeur and a hundred servants all falling out of the cupboards when I pulled a bell. If I wanted an acid drop,

I rang for a servant to bring it. Walden had to fight every inch of the way and his domestic needs are very working class. It sounds silly because people think there isn't a class system, but there is, and he's a primitive-type man. His roots, his mother and his background are very important to him. He's never really got away from them.'

The man she still calls Walden expected her to be a traditional wife but she had neither the inclination nor the temperament to be anything of the kind. 'He had no experience of upper-class women,' she told me.

> He wanted somebody who would stay at home and look after him. Our marriage was a great gamble and it didn't come off, though I've no regrets. He's not a nice man but I don't like nice men. We had a very intense life and it was worth it. Just after I left him he gave me a list of ladies he thought might be suitable for him to marry. He asked me to pick out the next wife. I thought it was extraordinary but he does do extraordinary things. He can't live alone, a lot of men can't. He can look after himself very well in life but not in the home. He can't put a light bulb in.

Like many ex-wives, Jane blames her ex-husband's mother for a lot of their problems:

> She wanted him to be a priest . She was determined to get him out of that environment of a desperately poor coal-mining area. She pushed him very hard. He was never allowed to be ill, never allowed to fail at anything. She was an extremely powerful, tyrannical woman. Brian's mother was everything to him and she died when he was

twelve. He wanted a wife who was like her and would always be there, devoting her life to him and cooking him egg and chips. There's a lot of truth in the theory that men marry their mothers. I couldn't be more different but his first and his third wife resemble his mother. I was an aberration.

If you're a working-class girl who wants to find an upper-middle-class chap, you would do well to study upper-middle-class women. They have a style and safe dress sense all their own which hasn't markedly changed in decades. Mummies and daughters have similar tastes and wear the kind of uniform loved by Tiggy Legge-Bourke. During the day, they have calf-length dark skirts with white shirts and sleeveless jerkins. They are fond of hair bands or silk scarves emblazoned with horses, which they wear tied on their chin. They are very attached to the pearl studs Daddy gave them for their twenty-first birthday and only ever wear medium-heeled shoes. In winter, they keep warm in guernseys with striped shirts underneath. They have strong hair, good skin, wear very little makeup and wouldn't be seen dead in false eyelashes. Many of them went to Cheltenham Ladies' College and their best friend in middle age is a girl who shared the same dorm. Their spiritual home is Peter Jones because it's where Nanny took them to buy their school uniform. Their heroines are Virginia Bottomley and Joanna Trollope and they think Princess Anne is the kind of good egg who would be a Trojan in a crisis. They have long, sturdy legs and their sensible, down-to-earth exteriors camouflage powerful libidos. They have a sneaking regard for Mrs Paddy Ashdown and Christine Hamilton because they stood by their chaps and never complained. They share Mrs

Hamilton's economical streak when it comes to saving string and not buying many clothes but those they do buy are expensive and more often than not from Jaegar.

If their son lets them down by marrying a working-class girl, they are appalled by her extravagant tastes and penchant for overpriced makeup. They've always sworn by Yardley and think you can't beat Johnson's baby oil as a remover for mascara. They are also horrified to see how much their beloved son helps out at home. 'My dear, he even gets up in the night when the baby cries,' they tell their friends. They are the kind of women who are terrific in a disaster and much more effective with a power drill than their husbands. They are brilliant at tapestry and always look tidy, even when nobody is there. They never slop around in dressing gowns. They believe in standards and Britain. They don't think of themselves as snobs but they wouldn't dream of calling their daily by her Christian name. Josceline Dimbleby, who is quintessentially upper middle, knew her former daily for nearly thirty years. There was little they didn't know about each other and, in fact, I think they loved each other but never once were they on first-name terms.

If you want to marry above your station and you are called Marlene or Tracey, I would change your name. House of Commons hooker Pamela Bordes changed her name to Pamella as she thought it would make her sound more interesting. She grew up in India and then came to England to make her fame and fortune. She worked as a prostitute in London but combined her professional existence with a private life which took her into the top echelons of society. Any ambitious, ruthless girl could learn a lot from Pamella. She said she came from a high-born Indian family but, as she was a pathological liar, this may or may not have been true.

She was shrewd, manipulative and resourceful. Her mother was ashamed of her daughter's lifestyle and Pamella told me she once said, 'We read of the Air India crash. We hoped you were on it.'

When she was invited to a grand dinner party, Pamella always asked for a copy of the guest list in advance. She would then look up the chaps in *Who's Who* and memorize the details. At dinner, she would make it quite clear to every male guest she talked to that she knew all about his illustrious career. He would be deeply impressed, bowled over by her intelligence and amazed that such a beauty could be so perceptive. She turned flattery into an art form. Having seen her in action, I can only say that laying it on with a trowel never failed. She knew that you can't over-egg the pudding when it comes to telling chaps how wonderful they are. She would do corny things like snaking up to a man, fingering his tie and saying, 'What a wonderful colour,' and he'd be putty in her hands. Jerry Hall employs the same technique but it's only effective when the perpetrator is alluring and utterly confident of her sexual allure.

Pamella fooled the shrewd journalist Andrew Neil who fell in love with her and came dangerously close to marrying her. The ex-editor of the *Observer* Donald Trelford was captivated and gave her a copy of his book inscribed 'To Pamella who snookered us all'. She was incredibly focused and once she had targeted her prey, nothing deflected her. She was a beautiful Indian girl so in Western eyes she was classless but it was her powerful sex appeal which opened every door.

Some time ago, I walked through Düsseldorf airport with her. She wore an old mackintosh and no makeup but, as she strode along, the heads of all chaps aged from fourteen to eighty whipped around to look at her. I staggered behind with all her luggage and finally she turned to me graciously and said, 'Lynda, I must help. Let me carry your handbag.' Her Achilles heel was her filthy temper, short fuse and vengeful nature. On one occasion, she broke into Andrew Neil's flat and slashed all his clothes. She was a monster to interview but she was absolute proof that sex appeal, ruthlessness and determination can take a working girl wherever she wants to go. The vital thing is to decide what you want.

The greatest disadvantage for any girl marrying into a different class is that her husband will assume that his opinions on décor, social life and bringing up children are the right ones. He will be so anxious his wife doesn't let him down that he will be critical and censorious. An upper-class man married to a working-class girl is forever waiting for her to do something vulgar and disgrace him. He will also be convinced that the way his mother organized things, be it the drawing room, the garden, the flowers or the daily, is the only way. Meanwhile, his mother will be so sure her daughter-in-law is going to be a disaster that she will interfere far too much. I once helped my mother-in-law make the beds and, afterwards, she said critically to my husband, 'Lynda doesn't even know how to do hospital corners.' Since I am not a trained nurse, this didn't seem shaming to me but she obviously thought that an upper-class girl would have learned hospital corners at her posh boarding school.

If you want to marry out of your class, the important thing is to decide whether or not the plus side outweighs the downside. I would recommend making a list of the potential advantages and the tricky areas. You may find that you will have to adopt a way of life that is alien to you. The way married couples live is still, to a certain extent, dictated by the job of the husband.

Model Bronwen Pugh, who was described by couturier Pierre Balmain as one of the most beautiful women he had ever met, married Bill Astor of the fabulously wealthy Astor family. He lived at Cliveden, the vast estate he'd inherited, where his powerful mother, Nancy, ruled as a political hostess for over three decades. The elegant bride was the middle-class daughter of a lawyer and, even on her wedding day, was savaged by her vitriolic mother-in-law. She wore a white ottoman silk coat with a matching bandeau tied around her head. 'I do wish she'd take that hat off,' announced Nancy to press photographers. 'Isn't it terrible? I can't think what made her wear it. It looks like an aircraft propeller.' She ordered her son to tell his bride to change before announcing loudly, 'Bronwen is not my cup of tea.'

If you are a chap who has married beneath him, my advice would be to never tell your wife what your mother has said about her, unless of course – and this is unlikely – it is flattering. The new Lady Astor had much to contend with, including the staff, who were feudal and had a tendency towards bossiness. Mr Lee, the butler, was a kind of real-life version of Mrs Danvers in the novel *Rebecca* and Viscountess Astor admits, 'There were times when I felt like the second Mrs de Winter.'

The butler ran Cliveden on oiled wheels and the exceedingly snobbish servants considered the new chatelaine to be a parvenue. She was not allowed to make any decisions for herself and brought only a few clothes and books when she moved into the house. Initially, she felt more of a guest than a hostess. Every morning, the maid came into her bedroom with the breakfast tray. She put the toothpaste on Lady Astor's toothbrush and selected the clothes she was expected to wear.

One day, Bronwen had the temerity to look in the large

fridge in the kitchen. The offended cook gave notice and the new Lady Astor conceded defeat. From then on, whenever she was asked anything by the butler or the housekeeper, she simply said, 'Whatever you think.' Now she reveals, 'I was always opening doors in the house and discovering rooms I had never seen before.'

Nancy Astor continued to be offensive and, today, Viscountess Astor says, 'She would stand over and needle me and try to find a way of making me burst into tears by saying rude things. She'd criticize my appearance and when I was pregnant she said, "What do you think you're doing marrying my son? You have no right to do this."' By instinct or chance, Bronwen decided that the only way to deal with such a mother-in-law is never to retaliate. You must never show that you mind and, in the end, they give up. It's a wise policy for any daughter-in-law. Although a chap may dislike his mother, he can't bear anyone else attacking her for being rude or a monster, as he feels it reflects on him. A lot of men and particularly those from the upper classes are quite incapable of telling their mothers what they really feel.

Angela Fox, of the famous theatrical Fox family, was married to London's leading theatrical agent Robin Fox, who was a handsome ex-Harrovian military hero. She said that he would talk affectionately to his mother on the telephone, then fling down the phone and say how much he loathed her. Angela was an arch snob but only about talent. She liked people who were, in her words, 'in the first eleven'. She used to say, 'I love the top people and I love chimney sweeps. I hate the middle lot.'

Her husband had an affair with the late Duchess of Kent, having told his wife soon after they married, 'You know I have no intention of being faithful to you. I shall sleep with whoever I like.' He kept his vow but the amour with the very grand Duchess was the one which hurt Angela most. 'She was odious,' she said. 'She was the most hateful of his mistresses. I never minded him going to bed with somebody, but one minds when they are taken away from you mentally. You mind the jokes they share, the friendship, that's much worse than the act of sex. But I'm a bit of a bitch. I was far from goody-goody. I used to see them off in my own way.'

Weddings, irrespective of class, are full of problems. At working-class weddings, the ornate invitations are covered in silver cupids and birds and include a present list with a note saying, 'Money would be very welcome.' The couple attempt to get as many presents as possible for the least amount of financial outlay. So they ask just a few guests to the church and wedding breakfast but then throw a rave-up in the evening for as many as they can cram into the British Legion Hall. The wedding breakfast takes place earlier in the bride's father's local, because the landlord gives him a cut-price deal. Guests are served with sparkling wine, cheese and pineapple on sticks, crisps and peanuts and later help themselves to a buffet of cold quiche and coleslaw. The bride's father makes a rambling speech, loses his notes and gets maudlin about 'my little lass'. The best man then tells dubious jokes about the bride being a right little goer and his wife looks stony-faced. Regrettably, too many best men ignore the sensible advice that jokes at a family wedding should not be crude, suggestive or contain cracks about the bridegroom's prowess as a stud. They definitely ought not to be culled from either Bernard Manning or Jim Davidson. They should be full of warmth, charm and flattery for the bride and her mother without an ounce of sexual innuendo.

In the evening, the bridal couple dance to music from a

disco and grow so amorous the guests fear that consummation is imminent. The wedding presents are all on display on a trestle table and include a Teasmade, a hostess trolley, tablemats with scenes of London landmarks and a cut-glass trifle bowl. By the time the karaoke gets going, most of the guests are inebriated and home truths are spoken never to be forgotten. The bride's mother gets tired and emotional and has to go and sit in the Ladies and slip off her stilettos. The bride goes to comfort her as the groom takes the opportunity to chat up the prettiest bridesmaid. Then he feels a few pangs of regret for his newly committed marital state and wonders if he's done the right thing.

Finally, they go off to the Barratt house they have just moved into and it takes the bride half an hour to take the hairpins out of her hair. This had been backcombed, swept up and lacquered till it set like concrete. By the time she has disassembled it and put on her honeymoon nighty, the bridegroom is asleep and snoring. She goes next door to ring her tired and emotional mother who says, 'I never thought he was good enough for you. But what can you expect with a mother like he's got?' At least they are both from the same social background so their rows will not be about manners, accents, irritating phrases, vulgarity or even sex.

The next morning, they go on their package holiday to Magaluf, better known as Blackpool in the sun. They stay at the Fiesta Jungla Hotel and drink a local cocktail which is so powerful one bar offers a free T-shirt and G-string to any customer who drinks five. They spend every afternoon on the beach and get so sunburned they wince every time they touch. This is much more sophisticated than in the old days when young, working-class couples were lucky to get a week in a caravan at Morecambe or Great Yarmouth.

Derek Hatton, former deputy leader of Liverpool City Council, and his wife, Shirley, spent their honeymoon in Shirley's mother's caravan along with Derek's parents. The wedding night was accompanied by a ribald running commentary from Mr Hatton senior. 'We laugh about it now,' says Mrs Hatton, who must have a saintly nature. Her husband has absolute confidence and aplomb. He is fazed by nobody although, if he were, he would never admit it, even to himself. He has the arrogance and self-assurance of any aristocrat. 'I've never been overawed by any individual,' he told me. 'First time I met Margaret Thatcher I thought, "You've got two eyes, a nose and a mouth. I've got the same. The only difference is, I'm better than you."'

On the day I met Mr Hatton, he was wearing an embroidered orange shirt, a diamond ring on his exquisitely manicured hands, a gold bracelet and a very sharp, expensive Italian suit. 'I know a man who gets them wholesale for footballers,' he said. Whatever he wants, one feels Mr Hatton would always know a man who could get it wholesale. He also feels that although everyone else has to die, he doesn't see why he should.

There is an increasing trend for couples from the affluent working class to get married in the Bahamas or on a beach in Jamaica. This is partly because it's one way of ensuring that the couple don't have to invite their parents. I am afraid this will normally result in the bridegroom's mother taking umbrage and accusing her daughter-in-law of being a spendthrift and throwing away good money on foreign nuptials. Be that as it may, the arrangement has become so popular that travel firms now do cut-price holidays in the sun with wedding arrangements thrown in.

Marriages which take place in Britain but away from the

bride's home usually mean that she's marrying upwards and doesn't want her in-laws to see where she comes from. Margaret Thatcher was the daughter of a Grantham grocer, and when she married the very middle-class Denis Thatcher, the wedding was understandably in London. They were snobbish times and it wasn't long after the young Ted Heath wrote to the *Daily Express* to say that his father was a builder not a carpenter.

Nothing reveals tensions in a family more than a wedding and lower-middle-class weddings are no exception. Professor Ray Bull, a psychologist at the University of Portsmouth, says, 'We are all two people, who we want to be and who we are. Adopting certain clothing is one of the easiest ways of making you feel more like your ideal self.' This doesn't work for me as I'm small and freckled and my ideal self is tall and thin with the kind of skin which never lets you down by turning bright red. Sadly, even the most expensive couture clothes can't do much about this problem. Wedding outfits are meant to show people at their best but a middle-class bride sometimes over-gilds the lily. She turns herself into a modern-day version of Cinderella at the ball, with such a full skirt she can scarcely get down the aisle. The bride's mother is so determined to outdo the mother of the bridegroom with the size of her hat that she looks like a parasol on legs. All future mothers-in-law turn into monsters prior to a wedding and the bridegroom increasingly grows apprehensive about her bossiness, her control freakery, her ruthless determination and the way she dominates his future father-in-law. Since the bridal couple are likely to be paying for part of the wedding, the bride runs around trying to save money and is on her knees by the week of the nuptials. She has a day of pampering in a health club and is so exhausted she cries the whole time. The emphasis is on doing the right thing. The bride's mother buys a book on etiquette and follows it to the letter. The book says that on invitations widows must be addressed as Mrs Jane Smith not Mrs John Smith. She insists on doing this and ends up offending all the older widows in both families, who are possessive about the name of their late husband.

The reception is held at a local hotel and the bride arrives at church in either a white Rolls or a horse-drawn carriage. The wedding cake has a model of a bride and groom on top and the bride is determined to exploit every moment of her starring role and behaves like Elizabeth Taylor on a bad-hair day. She's irritated when she sees how dreadful her two fat future sisters-in-law look in their peach-coloured bridesmaid outfits and snaps, 'God, you look like Pinky and Perky.' She has her hair done in such an elaborate style the main emotion of the bridegroom as he gets his first glimpse is one of sheer horror. He starts to wonder if he's making a terrible mistake. Also, he's feeling queasy as he still hasn't got over his stag night when his friends organized a stripper.

As the newlyweds come out of church, the guests throw highly coloured confetti, which infuriates the vicar. When they get to the hotel, the waitresses are holding trays of Spanish *cava* not champagne, which makes the bridegroom's smarter relations feel superior. When he gives his speech the bride's father foolishly tells a joke about his own wedding. 'It feels just like yesterday,' he says. 'I wish it was tomorrow and I'd cancel it.' He then catches sight of the murderous look on his wife's face which could fast-dry cement. 'Just joking, love,' he says, but it's too late.

Upper-middle-class weddings tend to be more chic and the bride's father will generally be paying most of the bill. The reception is held at a country hotel or at home and the bride's mother's friends strip their herbaceous borders to provide the flowers. If the reception is at the bride's house, her father may insist on Portaloos being erected in the garden. These were provided for the wedding of Jemima Goldsmith and Imran Khan and are naff beyond belief. I've even been to weddings where guests weren't allowed into the house as though they might be petty thieves or unwelcome intruders.

When a bride marries up, her relations are so intimidated and terrified of letting her down that they scarcely speak, but when a chap marries up, his family turn up for the wedding brimming with a kind of aggressive truculence.

At upper-class weddings, an expensive professional makeup artist does the bride's makeup and the perfectionist dress designer rearranges the frock as the bride goes into church. Since the only guests who aren't posh are the old nannies from both families, the bride isn't frightened that someone is going to let her down.

The service is often held in the church on the family estate with all the villagers turning up to see the show. The church is crammed with upper-class country-garden flowers like stocks, sweet peas, white roses and lavender, without a carnation in sight. The bride and bridegroom walk back to the marquee where a string quartet is playing. Handsome waiters in long white pinnies are holding trays of peach juice and champagne and there are smart canapés including *crostini* with roast Mediterranean vegetables, quail's eggs, salmon blinis and carpaccio on Parmesan biscuits.

The only discordant note is the bride's stepmother who is not much older than her stepdaughter. Unwisely, she's dressed to kill in something expensive from Versace which shows off her Bermuda tan and endless legs.

The seating plan, which is the only thing the bride and her mother have had to fix, has caused a few thundering rows. This is because the bride wants to keep her father happy by letting his second wife sit next to him. Her mother wants her to be seated on a table in the farthest corner next to the exit flap and the elderly sharp-tongued family nanny who can be relied upon to put her in her place. Before one very high-profile wedding the situation became so contentious that the sit-down lunch was scrapped and turned into a buffet. The seating plan is a nightmare. In fact, at my elder daughter's wedding, we had a row every time we tried to work it out. When a friend asked what I was going to throw at the bride, I could only think of bricks.

As fathers of upper-class brides usually have lots of land, the possibilities for a dramatic departure by the bride and groom are unlimited. One couple left by a boat moored on the river which ran through the family woods and another flew off from the helicopter pad where the family helicopter awaited. Stately homes don't necessarily ensure a glorious wedding which was proved by the nuptials of Earl Spencer. The rain poured relentlessly down when he married Victoria Lockwood, who looked like a bedraggled ghost. The nervous best man, Darius Guppy, failed to give his speech and the bride's middle-class family were all totally overawed by the aristocratic Spencers.

Marriage is always difficult but it's a damned sight harder if you come from different classes because there is no common ground. Family gatherings are hellish and there is absolutely no chance of the two sets of in-laws becoming friends. The person who suffers most, of course, is the husband or wife who has married into the higher social sphere. Christmas, above all, is a minefield and at least one bomb usually explodes. If a working-class girl has married up and organizes Christmas as her in-laws would do it, she makes her own parents feel uneasy. She feels torn in two, and by the end of Christmas is on her knees. Her in-laws almost certainly eat Christmas dinner in the evening but her parents prefer it midday. If everyone is staying in the house, one solution is to invite lots of other people in for meals as a kind of diversionary tactic. Then, when everyone arrives, the house will look festive and glorious but only because the hostess has been scurrying around like a workaholic skivvy since dawn. On Christmas Day, her parents will want to have a singsong around the piano and play noisy party games, which is anathema to her in-laws.

Since the two sets of in-laws share neither similar experiences, politics nor views, almost the only possible topic of conversation is the grandchildren. Even this can be fraught with danger as the maternal grandparents are loving, overprotective and indulgent. They are called Granny and Grandpa, love to see the grandchildren showing off and yearn only for them to be happy. They do not have rigid rules or timetables. The paternal grandparents are, by their own choice, called Grandmother and Grandfather and think discipline is close to godliness. They really do believe that children should be seen and not heard, which is inconceivable to a daughter-in-law who believes in the importance of self-expression.

I once said to the daughter of an earl who lived in a stately pile that it must have been wonderful growing up in such an historic house. 'It was horrible,' she said. 'We slept in the attics and were never allowed in the drawing room. At night the wind howled round the rafters, we were terrified and thought vampires were coming to get us.'

Upper-class children are rarely cosseted and their parents still have an old-fashioned belief that their place is out of sight and with Nanny. They employed nannies to bring up their own children and are saddened to observe that, by their standards, their slapdash daughter-in-law is a bit sluttish. I became so paranoid about putting things away in my mother-in-law's kitchen that one day I put the very valuable silver teapot into the fridge and she thought it had been stolen by burglars. Surveys have proved that when women marry men from a higher social stratum they are far more likely to make it work than men in similar situations. Women have the sense to do things someone else's way if it's going to give them a leg up the ladder. We look on it as improving ourselves not corrupting our souls.

12

CLASS IS HERE TO STAY

I began writing this book at a time when the popular myth was that the class war was dead. The reaction I got from many people was that the whole thing was absurd. 'You're writing a book about class?' they said, as though it was something archaic that they had vaguely heard of, like bear baiting. Since then, the subject has rarely been out of the news. The Chancellor of the Exchequer, Gordon Brown, spoke at a trade union reception and said, 'It's about time we had an end to the old Britain where all that matters is the privileges you were born with, rather than the potential you actually have.' He evoked ecstatic applause from his audience but his words stirred up a response which revealed the hypocrisy that exists in Britain today.

Class awareness, I suspect, is something most people are secretly conscious of but don't want to acknowledge. We do not live in a classless society and I am sure we never will, as class-consciousness and snobbery is an integral part of human nature.

Snobbishness is only dangerous when it blinds people to reality and makes them judge those they meet purely on their accents and possessions. Otherwise, it's rather a life-enhancing characteristic. After all, everyone is a snob about something, be it food, family, speech or where they live, because we all have different versions of what snobbery means.

Choice of words can be a total giveaway just as much as accents. Newsreader Kirsty Young is beautiful, stylish and married to a rich, middle-class husband. However, when she became pregnant, her working-class roots were touchingly revealed when she talked about being 'nine weeks gone' and 'in the family way'. My father could never bring himself to use the word 'homosexuals' and would always say, 'being the way they are'.

'A degree of snobbishness,' says Paul Johnson, 'is essential to novel-writing. All great novelists are and must be snobs. A novelist must have the ability to classify human beings into minutely differentiated categories which convey social, moral and aesthetic messages to the readers. It is one way in which characters are brought to life.' Mr Johnson was defending snobbish Anthony Powell who was obsessed with genealogy. Mr Powell wrote about what he called 'smart people', which, since he was absolutely socially secure, meant the people in his own social circle. Nevertheless, he did say, 'To underline the fallibility of such judgements it should be added that someone staying with Gerry Wellington (7th Duke) was unwise enough to refer to a woman they both knew as "smart". Gerry drew in his breath slightly, "A nice woman, certainly. But smart? I don't recollect ever having seen her at the Sutherlands' or the Ancasters'."'

I have always used the word 'posh' rather than 'smart' but a friend of mine said, 'That's terribly vulgar, or are you using it ironically?' I lied and said, 'Yes,' whereupon she heaved a sigh of relief and said, 'Oh well, that's all right then.'

The socially ambitious Sir David Frost believes that the class war continues to thrive and flourish in the City. His production company made the film *Rogue Trader* about the Barings Bank scandal. Sir David met Nick Leeson when he was in prison in Hong Kong and says, 'It was clear that, had he been called Nicholas *Fothering* Leeson, he'd have been at Ford Open Prison. Instead he was hung out to dry.' Nick Leeson grew up on a Watford council estate but many posher names involved in the scandal totally escaped blame.

America is frequently praised as a meritocracy without an atom of class-consciousness but this is far from the truth. I went as a journalist on a trip organized by the travel company Abercrombie & Kent. It was a week's upmarket train tour through the South of France with overnight stays at various grand hotels. It was the kind of gracious train travelling done by rich Victorians. Everything was arranged in advance, luggage was taken care of and transport awaited outside every station to take us to our hotel for dinner.

Apart from me and one Englishman, all the other travellers were American. It very quickly became obvious that the class system certainly does exist in the USA. There was a man, his wife and his mother from downtown New York, who had made their money out of running hot-dog stands. Also, there was a wealthy East Coast lawyer and his wife, with his parents. The two groups avoided each other and clearly did not want to be associated in any way. The lawyer didn't exactly say, 'You don't expect to meet vulgar people like that on a trip like this,' but it was obviously how he felt. Within days, the lawyer and his family and an American general and his wife had become the unspoken leaders of the group and, indisputably, they were seen as the élite. The courier said that, on every trip, a similar pattern always evolved as natural leaders emerged.

American movie star Kirk Douglas is a man who knows much about class-consciousness in his adopted country. He is the son of Russian immigrants and was born Issur

Danielovitch. He grew up in searing poverty in downtown New York and, despite fame, wealth and success, his gnawing insecurity never totally left him. Even at the height of his career, he remained suspicious and a loner, always trying to prove he was better than everyone and never quite believing it. 'Anger kept me going,' he said to me when I interviewed him in Beverly Hills. 'Anger fuelled my life.'

Mr Douglas is absolute proof that the effects of our childhood never leave us. 'I've had an iron discipline which comes from fear, fear of failure, fear of rejection,' he added. 'I've never completely grown up but that's being an actor. Every artist must retain a certain childishness and young Issur is still deep in my guts. I have mixed feelings about him. I am ashamed of him and I am proud of him, but he's part of me. He's the force which gave me whatever talent and ambition I have.' He also told his sons that they didn't have the advantages he'd had because poverty and deprivation had been his driving force. Equally, Sean Connery used to take his son, Jason, to the Gorbals to see the slums where he had grown up, and whenever I go to Lancashire, I drive round the council estate of my youth.

I was halfway through writing this book when my father died. I had been thinking so much about him and the way class had affected his life. He grew up in poverty but with a burning ambition to succeed. An academic friend once said, 'Norman has a brilliant but untrained mind.' Only two days before his death, he was still refining the golf-swing machine he'd invented. Over the years he'd spent a fortune on patents but he never faltered in his conviction that one day it would become a world-wide success and he would be a billionaire.

When he suddenly became ill, I drove from London to Lancashire late one Sunday evening. The journey seemed endless but I finally arrived. He was in bed being looked after by his loving neighbours who are proof that in this sometimes disturbing world goodness still exists. He seemed to have slightly recovered and we talked about the party we were planning for his birthday on 4 April. Around midnight, I said goodnight and went to sleep in my old childhood bedroom. I left the light on and said, 'Just call if you need me, Daddy.'

At one-thirty, I woke and there was an extraordinary stillness in the house. I went to see him and he had died. He looked at peace and later I discovered that he had left everything in immaculate order, including a letter addressed to me saying, 'There is nothing but love in this house for you.' He also said, 'The patents on the machine *must* be kept up.' In the week before his death, he had washed everything in the house, including all the blankets. I found two huge boxes in which he had saved every article I'd ever written as well as all the letters and postcards I'd sent him over the years. Immediately, my three children travelled north to be with me. We sat weeping together in my father's house where every wall is covered with pictures of all of us going back over thirty years.

We planned his funeral which was to be in Leigh Parish Church where I was christened and married. It was a celebration of my father's life and the church was packed with family and friends. Initially, I didn't know whether or not to include his date of birth on the order of service because he was always touchy about his age. He rarely admitted to more than sixty-nine. In fact he was eighty-nine but emotionally he was about thirty; in his spirit he was twenty-seven and in his loving heart he was ageless. He had just got a new computer and was looking forward to going on the Internet. He was the supreme example of how not to grow old despite the passing of the years. I gave the address and spoke about him and my mother. He'd never got over her death but he didn't let it defeat or destroy him. I said that after the service we would drive Norman to the cemetery to be with Peggy once more.

We went in convoy and, in the age-old ceremony, threw earth on to his coffin as it was lowered into the grave. We then drove back to his house without him and did what he loved, which was to open a few bottles of wine. I only regret that I didn't get champagne because my father adored champagne. The man who had grown up in a two-up, two-down terrace in a bleak Lancashire street loved luxury and posh hotels. 'Just to the top, love,' he said at Christmas as I filled his glass.

I was sad that I hadn't told him that I was doing a book on class and that I was going to dedicate it to him and my mother. Writing this book has, in many ways, sorted me out and brought me to my senses. It has made me realize how fortunate I was as a child and what is important. I was given a great sense of my own worth and dignity and this stands any of us in good stead.

There were so many things I wanted to ask my father about his early life. Now it's too late and I'm full of anguish and regret and a desperate desire to have just one more chance to tell him how proud I was of him. I was always so concerned with getting on myself that I never took the time to value what he had achieved. 'He was a good age,' people say but he'd always been so vibrant and strong and such a powerful influence that I'd been lulled into a feeling of false security. I thought he would always be there with his loving, selfless support. He had exceptionally high standards of morality. He was literally incapable of telling a lie. He never let me down and now I feel bereft. He had a passionate faith in the valour and dignity of the old working classes. He'd always voted

Labour but he had grave fears about New Labour. He was worried by their arrogance, their desire to control people and their inherent belief that they know what is best for us. He thought they were patronizing and without respect for the dignity of the working man.

New Labour leaders have become a class of their own and the hierarchy are just as isolated from the common herd as the old-fashioned aristocrats. They are an educated élite who believe they are born to rule and expect to be obeyed not challenged.

Baroness Jay is the daughter of Lord Callaghan and has rollercoastered her way through life on a sea of privilege with obvious disdain for anyone she thinks is her intellectual inferior. Her children were all privately educated. She went to a direct-grant school but called it 'a pretty standard grammar school' and she is opposed to privilege for anyone else. She is proof that a ruling class will always emerge, whether it's based on birth, inheritance, wealth, power or class.

It's impossible for human beings to be totally equal without the balance of power tilting in one direction or the other. Britain remains class-ridden in spite of New Labour's claims about creating a one-nation society. In the year 2000, a MORI poll found that most people believe that the Labour Government has failed to reduce class divisions, and a quarter think that they have actually grown.

John Prescott, Labour's Deputy Leader, drones on about class warfare but lives like a lord. He was once described as 'a big ego, difficult to work with and a graduate whose sentences sound the same when spoken backwards or forwards'. He went to Ruskin College, Oxford, and spends weekends at the luxurious, twenty-one-roomed mansion Dorneywood in Buckinghamshire which and has nine bathrooms and a butler. At the 1999 Party Conference, having told the rest of us to walk rather than use the car, Mr Prescott was driven the few yards from his hotel to the conference centre. New Labour political soirées in elegant London drawing rooms, open only to the chosen, are just as élitist as the old-fashioned gentleman's clubs. The foot soldiers of old Labour have never felt more isolated, adrift or despised. At party conferences in the old days they were a powerful presence. Sadly, there is little place for them in the slick orchestrated events that are now run more for show than debate.

The worst thing the Labour Government did in the seventies, when Harold Wilson was Prime Minister, was to abolish grammar schools in their so-called quest for equality. Historically, grammar schools provided stepping-stones for working-class children. Those who didn't pass the scholar-ship went to what were called technical schools, which were a wonderful training for those with practical skills. The majority of the children in my form at grammar school came from working-class families. Most of us had parents who wanted us to achieve what had been denied to them. None of us believed that our backgrounds would be of any disadvantage when it came to applying for university. Every pupil in my year who wanted to go to university did so. They included one girl who lived in such dire poverty that there were only ragged blankets to sit on in the front room of her house and upstairs there were just mattresses on the floors. But she went on to become a headmistress.

The basic question about class is whether birth or money defines your status. The upper classes, on the whole, stick together. They, in common with the rich, famous and powerful, are appalled when they are treated like everyone else. This was gloriously demonstrated on Millennium Eve when VIPs were horrified at being forced to queue at the Dome along with the 'ordinary people', as Lord Falconer calls us. The élite think that queuing, being told there is no spare table in a restaurant or travelling by tube are not experiences they should ever have to endure. They were not only appalled, they were amazed. They were being asked momentarily to lead the kind of lives other people lead. One definition of a snob is somebody who believes he or she merits special treatment. They pander to the whims of those they see as socially superior to themselves but are indifferent to those they perceive as beneath them.

I had lunch with former royal butler Paul Burrell just before his book on entertaining was published. We each had a glass of champagne and I stretched out my own glass to clink against his to say, 'Here's to the book.' I know clinking glasses is naff but it was meant as a joke. Paul was just about to do the same when a look of horror and revulsion crossed his face. He imperceptibly lifted his glass, keeping it close to his chest and said, 'No. This is how we do it at Kensington Palace.' He'd be aghast if he ever saw me drinking champagne with my children because we all clink glasses and then say, 'Cheers *bonjour.*' I know it's vulgar but I don't care, although when I told one of my daughters that I was going to mention it in the book, she said, 'You will explain why won't you?' It began as a joke years ago when we were on holiday in France and has now become a kind of good-luck ritual. We've done it on birthday celebrations at the Savoy and the Ritz and no doubt elicited a *frisson* of distaste from onlookers.

Of course, we all have double standards and I have to admit that if ever I see other people clinking glasses, my lip curls in contempt. This is one of the advantages of snobbery as there is nothing more satisfying than feeling superior. The first thing I do when I get any invitation is to run my fingers over the wording to make sure it's embossed. I'm very snooty about people who put covers on the arms of chairs, drink sweet sherry, have hostess trolleys, net curtains, electric fires with false flames, or call friends of their parents 'Aunty' and 'Uncle'.

The aristocracy have always got on well with the working class and the Duke of Devonshire insists that his valet Henry is a great friend. 'He's been with me for thirty-five years. He knows what I want before I do. If someone's coming who has given me something, a handkerchief or cufflinks, he puts them out for me to wear. People who don't have servants don't realize that they are part of the family.' Having said this, he adds that, on his mother's side, he is a Cecil and the Cecils are High Church and convinced the aristocracy knows best. On his father's side, he is a Cavendish and says the Cavendishes are very much in favour of improving the lot of the underprivileged, providing it doesn't interfere with their own wealth. 'Compassion without sacrifice' might be a more appropriate family motto for the Cavendish family than their current one which is 'Secure by caution'. The Duke lives at Chatsworth and is a keen racegoer. 'Racing is important to the English,' he says, 'and it's open to everybody. As the saying goes, "On the turf and under it, all men are equal."'

If you are used to being looked after by a valet, it's quite difficult to cope or make decisions on your own. Apparently, the current Duke of Marlborough gets in a terrible state if he has to go away without his valet and is forever asking his wife which tie he should wear. When Prince Charles went on a four-day retreat to Greece he took thirty items of luggage. 'He didn't have his valet to do his clothes so he took everything,' said a caustic friend.

One area where the upper and working classes differ

totally is in their attitude to nudity. Despite having slept with hundreds of willing girls before his second marriage, Bill Wyman hated them to see him without clothes on. 'Whenever I spent a first night with a lady,' he told me, 'it was always me saying, "Switch off the light."' The upper classes by comparison are unconcerned. 'Everyone always strips off at Hunt balls,' says Jilly Cooper, 'so you just grow up with it. A friend of mine went to a dinner party in Gloucestershire where everyone was stark-naked and she had a super time.'

Lady Celestria Noel agrees and makes it quite clear that it's a class issue. 'The upper classes have always had a very frank attitude to nudity,' she says, 'and being body-shy is considered terribly common. Country girls of a certain background tend to be terrifyingly confident. When I was coming out in the 1970s, I was always amazed at how ready everyone was to take their clothes off. Debs' dances invariably ended with skinny-dipping in the pool.'

Indeed, the Beaufort Hunt have produced a cookbook illustrated with pictures of themselves with nothing on and entitled *In the Buff*. Lady Katherine Howard, the daughter of the Earl of Suffolk, is one of the models and Prince Charles contributed a recipe for dressed artichoke soufflé. His views on nudity aren't known but, as he's a top toff, I assume he's fairly relaxed about stripping off, having endured all those cold showers at Gordonstoun. Presumably, public school robs the shyest people of embarrassment. Fifty years ago, upper-crust Harrovians swam in the school pool without swimsuits and there were no doors on the lavatories. When Patrick Lichfield revealed this to one of the working-class models posing for his glamour calendar, she asked, 'How did you get in?'

Grammar-school boys are much more modest and satirist, actor and writer John Cleese says, 'The first time I had to drop my knickers in front of a film crew it was like going through the sound barrier. I suppose my background in Weston-super-Mare was lower middle class. Mum had a very middle-class accent, she used to say "Orf", and Dad did the *Daily Telegraph* crossword, but basically he sold life insurance from his Austin 10.'

I don't even like communal changing rooms in dress shops, and when I was growing up I wore not only a vest but what was called a liberty bodice, destined to keep the northern chill out of one's bones. I belong to the Alan Bennett school of inhibition. Writing about going backstage after a show to congratulate the leading actor, he said, 'You knock on the door and are told to come in. You do so and find someone extremely famous in a state of considerable undress. It is a fact that very few leading actors are in the least bit self-conscious. Speaking as one who can scarcely remove his tie without first having a police cordon thrown round the building, I find this unselfconsciousness very disconcerting.'

I shouldn't think liberty bodices exist any more but in those days we didn't have central heating and David Blunkett told me that the only double glazing in his bedroom at his family's Sheffield council house was when the ice formed in winter on the other side of the window. 'I used to get out of bed and run for the nearest warm part of the house,' he said, 'before risking having a wash and going to the outside toilet.'

The subtitle of this book is 'How to Beat the British Class System' and there is no doubt that it can be beaten. The system only defeats people who are phoneys or frightened or ashamed. My insecure years were when I was trying to pretend to be something I wasn't. If this goes on for too long it can be crucifying as John Morgan found out. He was author of *Debrett's New Guide to Etiquette and Modern Manners* and he

wrote a weekly column in *The Times* under the heading 'Morgan's Modern Manners'. Every week he provided the answers to social dilemmas, from how to get guests to leave, to what to wear at a polo match or how to cope with spilt wine on a restaurant tablecloth. 'Insouciance is called for,' was Mr Morgan's response to the latter dilemma. But his huge postbag proved how much people still care about doing the right thing and he had a considerable following.

On the surface, Mr Morgan appeared to be a man who had everything – looks, style and panache. He cashed his cheques at Claridge's and Fortnum & Mason was his corner shop. He was a regular guest at the smartest parties and many people assumed he'd been educated at Eton. John Morgan actually went to a comprehensive school in Tadcaster and later reinvented himself as gentleman about town. He became detached from the life of his youth, and earlier this year he was believed to have committed suicide, though an open verdict was recorded. The deputy headmaster of his old school said, 'I presume that he didn't want his London friends to know that he was at a comprehensive. He must have thought it wasn't socially acceptable. He had recreated himself and I am so delighted that he made something of himself. But perhaps there is only so long you can live that life. A life so very different to your past.' In fact, there is no problem in living a new life as long as you are not trying to pretend the old one never existed. Fooling ourselves is the real danger.

This is a mistake Jimmy Savile never made. He is a dignified, remarkable, self-made man who is at ease in any social setting from Buckingham Palace to Blackpool Pier. He was the youngest of seven children in a materially deprived family. His first job as a teenager was as a coal miner and he has a vivid recollection of the day that he knew he wasn't going to work down the pit all his life. He was standing in the dawn bus queue with a group of fellow miners. It was pitch-dark and freezing cold. The bus stop was near some cross-roads and, as Jimmy waited, a black Bentley drew up at the traffic lights. 'It was driven by a lad,' he says, 'who was obviously coming home from a party because he was wearing evening dress with a white silk scarf. He wasn't much older than me and he was only fourteen feet away. I was filled with absolute joy. I was on my way to work, to a one-pound-and-five-pence-a-week job. I thought, "What I want is only fourteen feet away from me. I can travel that distance. I don't know how or when but I'm going to do it."'

Fifty years later, Jimmy Savile is a regular visitor to Highgrove, Chequers and Downing Street. He is known as the only man who can tease Margaret Thatcher. In 1990, he was knighted for his charity work. Sir James has travelled a lot further than fourteen feet. I wonder what happened to the privileged young man in the white silk scarf?

Recently somebody said to me, 'You come from nothing, Lynda, don't you?' It sounded more offensive than was intended and, presumably, meant that my family had no titles, no land and no social position. However, I had love, support, laughter and emotional security. I was imbued with the belief that I was inferior to no one and that anything could be achieved. 'You're as good as the Queen,' my grandfather, who worked down the pit all his life, used to say. The philosophy that everyone should be treated with civility and respect regardless of who they are was instilled in me. I also learned from the example of my fiendishly hard-working, proud parents that, if you are born into a working-class family in Lancashire, everything has to be earned but anything is possible. That seems to me to be a valuable lesson.